EPISODES OF THE END

The Revelation of Jesus Christ

Dr. Guy Lee

© Guy Lee 2020
by
Dr. Guy Lee
37 Bill Presley Road
Cleveland, Georgia 30528
Phone: 706-865-4555
E-mail: tometterlee@gmail.com

ISBN: 978-1-7344467-8-4

All rights reserved.
Printed in the United States of America

All Scripture quotations and references are from the
King James Version of the Holy Bible.

Published by
The Old Paths Publications
142 Gold Flume Way
Cleveland, GA 30528
www.theoldpathspublications.com
TOP@theoldpathspublications.com

Cover and Book Design by Linda E. Etterlee

DEDICATION

I want to thank all my family and friends for their prayers, encouragement, and support during the undertaking of writing this book. I want to specifically thank the following for their help:

- To my daughter, Linda, who typed the book

- To the following individuals for proofreading the book:
  - My wife, Adell
  - My daughters, Linda Etterlee and Beverly Jones
  - My son-in-laws, Tom Etterlee and Brad Jones
  - Rex Chosewood
  - Leah Chosewood
  - Brandon Chosewood
  - Brett Chosewood

This book is dedicated to all the Churches
of whom I served as Pastor.

Dr. Guy Lee
March 2020

FOREWORD

It is a great honor to be asked to write the foreword to these outlines and notes on the Book of Revelation, by Rev. Guy Lee. A man who though small in physical stature, has stood tall in the ministry of Lord and Savior Jesus Christ.

Guy answered the Lord's call to preach the Gospel in the year 1950 and began his ministry during the time when tent revivals were going strong. He has served as a full time Evangelist, then part time Pastor and finally full time Pastor, serving some fourteen (14) Churches.

Guy's many experiences over the years, coupled with his godly wisdom and compassion, led him into a unique ministry of being a "spiritual father" to multitudes of young preachers starting their ministries, including myself. He has truly been a Paul to many Timothys, unselfishly sharing his pulpit, providing opportunities to preach, helping in selecting good Bible commentaries, sermon resources and sermon preparation, or offering guidance, or just a word of encouragement and prayer.

His love for serious, in depth Bible study is revealed in his expository style of preaching and teaching, and in the tremendous library of Bible commentaries and reference works, he has acquired over the years.

These outlines and notes are the result of Guy having preached and taught the Book of Revelation numerous times, in many Churches. They are distinctly fundamental, conservative, pre-tribulational, and pre-millennial. I know they will be a valuable study tool for preachers, Sunday School teachers and laymen also, and will greatly help in grasping the big picture of the prophecies of this blessed book. May God give this labor the circulation it deserves.

– Rev. Rex Chosewood

TABLE OF CONTENTS

DESCRIPTION	PAGE

Dedication..3

Foreword..4

Table of Contents...5

Introduction..7

Chapter 1...8 - 26

      Church History Portrayed..23 - 26

Chapter 2...27 - 43

Chapter 3...44 - 68

      Daniel's Seventy Weeks..61 - 68

Chapter 4...69 - 75

Chapter 5...76 - 82

Chapter 6...83 - 90

Chapter 7...91 - 100

Chapter 8...101 - 105

Chapter 9...106 - 113

Chapter 10...114 - 119

Chapter 11...120 - 127

Chapter 12...128 - 134

Chapter 13...135 - 144

Chapter 14...145 - 152

EPISODES OF THE END, THE REVELATION OF JESUS CHRIST

Chapter 15..153 - 157

Chapter 16..158 - 164

Chapter 17..165 - 173

Chapter 18..174 - 182

Chapter 19..183 - 191

Chapter 20..292 - 200

Chapter 21..201 - 210

Chapter 22..211 - 219

A Word from the Author..220 - 221

INTRODUCTION

It has been my joy to deliver messages on the book of Revelation of Jesus Christ to many Churches. I always receive a great blessing from the fresh study of this closing portion of God's Word. Likewise, everyone who has studied this book has received a great blessing. That is a promise in this great book from God.

For many years, I have been asked by many of my friends and family to write down the messages and insight that God has given me of the book of Revelation. These outlines and studies are the things that God has helped me to understand in the study of Revelation. I am also indebted to those who have labored in the study of the book of Revelation before me.

I pray that this book will please the Lord and that He will use it for the edification of everyone that reads it and that it will be used to His honor and glory. The last prayer of Revelation is also my prayer, "The grace of our Lord Jesus Christ be with you all. Amen."

– Guy Lee

Revelation – Chapter 1

Revelation means unveiling, to take off the cover, or to reveal.

The Things Which Thou Hast Seen

I. **THE THEME – vs. 1-2**
    a. ***"THE Revelation of Jesus Christ, which God gave unto Him, to shew unto His servants things which must shortly come to pass; and He sent and signified it by his angel unto His servant John:"* - vs. 1**
    b. The Revelation of Jesus Christ which God gave to Him
        1. God gave the Revelation to Christ
        2. Christ in turn gave it to His angel
        3. The angel communicated it to John
        4. John then recorded what he received for the enlightenment of believers (his servants). The word "shortly" means rapidity of execution when action once begins. "Servant" means bondslave.
    c. The Testimony of John – **vs. 2**
        1. ***"Who bare record of the word of God, and of the testimony of Jesus Christ, and of all things that he saw." – vs. 2***
        2. The testimony of John is that he both "heard" and "saw". He "heard" the voices and "saw" the visions of this book.

II. **THE TIME IS AT HAND – vs. 3**
    a. *"Blessed is he that readeth, and they that hear the words of this prophecy, and keep those things, which are written therein: for the time is at hand."* – vs. 3
        1. In verse one (1) we have the "Revelation"
        2. In verse two (2) we have the "Record"

3. In verse three (3) we have the "Reading"
b. ***"Blessed is he that readeth"***
   1. Blessed means happy, well off, fortunate, supremely blessed
   2. Blessing on:
      - The one who reads it publicly
      - They that hear
      - They that keep it's sayings ("keep" means to guard with care)
c. ***"Time is at hand"***
   1. The word "time" denotes a space of time, a season. It can be a short time as in **Luke 4:5**, or a long time as in **Luke 8:27**. The statement "the time is at hand" does not mean that all the events in the Revelation were to come to pass within a short space of time in John's day. The length of the season is not stated. It means that their nearness should be kept in mind, as if they are imminent as a reminder to be prepared for what is to come.
   2. The fixed season is related to the time of Christ's second coming. Although Christ instructs people not to set dates concerning His coming, He did warn them to be prepared in **Matthew 24:36, 42, and 44**.

Salutation to the Churches

III. <u>THE TROUBLED CHURCHES</u> – vs. 4, 11-20, & Chapters 2 and 3

a. *"JOHN to the seven churches which are in Asia: Grace be unto you, and peace, from Him which is, and which was, and which is to come; and from the seven Spirits which are before His throne;"* - vs. 4
b. Some of these churches had trouble because they disobeyed God. Others had trouble because of persecution from the world.
   1. *"Grace"* is the source of our salvation.

    2. *"Peace"* is the result of God's grace
    3. *"Grace"*, *"Peace"*, and mercy are from Him *"which is"*, *"which was"*, and *"which is to come"*.
  c. The Trinity Described – **vs. 4**
    1. *"Which is"* implies independent, unchangeable, existence.
    2. *"Which was"* intimates God's relation to the past.
    3. *"Which is to come"* shows His connection to the future.
  d. **"and from the seven Spirits which are before His throne" – vs. 4**
    1. **Isaiah 11:2 "And the spirit of the LORD shall rest upon him, the spirit of wisdom and understanding, the spirit of counsel, and might, the spirit of knowledge and of the fear of the LORD:"**
    2. Seven denotes fullness and completeness.
    3. The seven Spirits is a reference to the sevenfold work of the Holy Spirit as revealed in **Isaiah 11:2** where He is called "the Spirit of the Lord", "the Spirit of Wisdom", "the Spirit of Understanding", "the Spirit of Counsel", "the Spirit of Might", "the Spirit of Knowledge", and "the Spirit of fear of the Lord".
    4. The term "seven spirits" does not mean there are seven Holy Spirits, but rather, it means the seven ministries of the Holy Spirit.
    5. When our Lord returns to sit upon David's throne, the Spirit will rest upon Him in His governmental office in exactly a sevenfold way.

IV. THE SON'S SACRIFICIAL SUFFERING – vs. 5
  a. **"And from Jesus Christ, who is the faithful witness, ..." - vs. 5**
    1. **"The faithful witness"** describes Christ's relationship to God while He was here on earth. As a true prophet, He never failed to declare the whole counsel of God.

2. The word "witness" means someone who sees, knows, and then speaks, and is a characteristic word of John. He uses it over seventy (70) times in his writings.
- b. *"... and the first begotten of the dead, ..."* - vs. 5
  1. Christ is both first-fruit and first-born of the dead.
     - As first-fruit, He is the first in time of the coming harvest of those who sleep in Jesus. See **I Corinthians 15:20-23**.
     - As first-born, it signifies that He is first in rank of all who will rise from the dead.
- c. *"... and the prince of the kings of the earth. ..."* - vs. 5
  1. This refers to His future rule over the earth.
  2. ***Isaiah 9:7** "Of the increase of his government and peace there shall be no end, upon the throne of David, and upon his kingdom, to order it, and to establish it with judgment and with justice from henceforth even for ever. The zeal of the LORD of hosts will perform this."*
- d. *"Unto Him that loved us ..."* - vs. 5
  1. The present love
- e. *"... and washed us from our sins in His own blood."* – vs. 5
  1. The past washing

V. THE SAINTS MINISTERING – vs. 6
- a. *"And hath made us kings and priests unto God and his Father; to Him be glory and dominion for ever and ever. Amen."* – vs. 6
- b. The Believer-Priest responsibility.
  1. To intercede on behalf of others
  2. To sympathize with his fellowman in their infirmities
  3. To supply the help required in time of need
     - If every Believer-Priest of today were functioning, as they should, how different the church would be.

- At the realization of all that He had done, the cry rang out; *"To Him be glory and dominion for ever and ever. Amen."*

VI. THE SECOND COMING – vs. 7

a. ***"Behold, He cometh with clouds; and every eye shall see Him, and they also which pierced Him: and all kindreds of the earth shall wail because of Him. Even so, Amen." – vs. 7***

1. This is not a reference to the rapture of the church, but to Christ's second coming in **Revelation 19:11-20**.

b. There are two (2) stages of Christ's coming:

1. He comes in the air for His saints
   - *John 14:3 "And if I go and prepare a place for you, I will come again, and receive you unto Myself; that where I am, there ye may be also."*
   - *Philippians 3:20 "For our conversation is in heaven; from whence also we look for the Savior, the Lord Jesus Christ:"*
   - *I Thessalonians 4:15-17 " (15) For this we say unto you by the word of the Lord, that we which are alive and remain unto the coming of the Lord shall not prevent them which are asleep. (16) For the Lord Himself shall descend from heaven with a shout, with the voice of the archangel, and with the trump of God: and the dead in Christ shall rise first: (17) Then we which are alive and remain shall be caught up together with them in the clouds, to meet the Lord in the air: and so shall we ever be with the Lord."*
   - *I Corinthians 15:23 "But every man in his own order: Christ the first-fruits; afterward they that are Christ's at His coming."*

2. He comes back to the earth with His Saints

- *Revelation 19:11-16 "(11) And I saw heaven opened, and behold a white horse; and He that sat upon Him was called Faithful and True, and in righteousness He doth judge and make war. (12) His eyes were as a flame of fire, and on His head were many crowns; and He had a name written that no man knew, but He Himself. (13) And He was clothed with a vesture dipped in blood: and His name is called The Word of God. (14) And the armies which were in heaven followed Him upon white horses, clothed in fine linen, white and clean. (15) And out of His mouth goeth a sharp sword, that with it He should smite the nations: and He shall rule them with a rod of iron: and He treadeth the winepress of the fierceness and wrath of Almighty God. (16) And He hath on His vesture and on His thigh a name written, KING OF KINGS, AND LORD OF LORDS."*

3. There is a seven (7) year tribulation period between these two events.
   - His first coming for the church (the rapture)
   - The seven (7) year tribulation period
   - His second coming to the earth – *Revelation 19:11-21*

VII. THE SUPREME SOVEREIGN – vs. 8

a. *"I am Alpha and Omega, the beginning and the ending, saith the Lord, which is, and which was, and which is to come, the Almighty." – vs. 8*

   1. The words "Alpha" and "Omega" are the first and last letters of the Greek alphabet.
   2. Christ is all that has gone before, all that is occurring, and that will occur which is now in it's final stage.

b. *"which is" – vs. 8*

   1. His absolute present existence

c. ***"which was"* – vs. 8**
      1. His former revelations of Himself and purpose
      2. He was the author of the purpose and program of Israel and the nations. He will also be the finisher.
   d. ***"which is to come"* – vs. 8**
      1. He is ready to make good all that He has spoken about in the future.
         - ***"the Almighty"* – vs. 8** and His eyes were as a flame of fire;"
      2. Almighty means the all-ruling. This is God as absolute and universal sovereign.
      3. He is the one who has dominion over all things, the one who controls all things, and the one who holds all things in His grasp.

The Patmos Vision

VIII. THE TRIBULATION – vs. 9-11
   a. *"I John, who also am your brother, and companion in tribulation, and in the kingdom and patience of Jesus Christ, was in the isle that is called Patmos, for the word of God, and for the testimony of Jesus Christ." –* **vs. 9**
   b. Companionship
      1. He is identified here as the one who has companionship with others which always has it's foundation in Christ, and which is in fellowship with Him. It is companionship in tribulation. This is not the *"great tribulation"* spoken of in **Matthew 24:21-29**. Christians are by no means exempt from tribulation. Jesus warned believers in the world *"ye shall have tribulation"*, **John 16:33**. The Apostle Paul said, **"we must through much tribulation enter into the Kingdom of God"**, **Acts 14:22**.
      2. John had been banished by the Roman government to the Isle of Patmos located in the Mediterranean Sea just off the mainland of

Asia, for the word of God and the testimony of Jesus Christ.
- c. Communion
  1. ***Revelation 1:10 "I was in the Spirit on the Lord's day, and heard behind me a great voice, as of a trumpet,"***
  2. ***"I was in the Spirit"***
     - John was communing with God
  3. ***"The Lord's Day"***
     - There is difference of opinion on the phrase, "The Lord's Day". Some hold it to mean the first day of the week (Sunday). Others believe that John, "in the Spirit" was carried forward to "the day of the Lord". "The day of the Lord" includes the seven (7) year period of tribulation Judgements on the earth (see **Daniel 9:24-25 and Matthew 24:15-30)**, the Millennial Reign of Christ on earth and Satan's last rebellion, **Revelation 20:10**.
     - Without being dogmatic, I personally believe it was the first day of the week (Sunday). However, either or both may be correct.
  4. ***"and heard behind me a great voice, as of a trumpet,"***
     - The trumpet emphasized authority, solemnity, alarm, or gladness. See **Numbers 10:1-10**, **Leviticus 25:8-24**, **Matthew 24:31**, **I Corinthians 15:52**, and **I Thessalonians 4:16**.
  5. ***"voice, as of a trumpet"***
     - This is the voice of Christ.
     - Recognized by the Saints
       1. ***John 10:4 "And when he putteth forth his own sheep, he goeth before them, and the sheep follow him: for they know his voice."***
     - Testing Men's Lives
       1. ***John 18:37 "Pilate therefore said unto Him, Art thou a king***

then? Jesus answered, Thou sayest that I am a king. To this end was I born, and for this cause came I into the world, that I should bear witness unto the truth. Every one that is of the truth heareth my voice."

- Warning Sinners
    1. *Acts 9:1-5* " *[1] And Saul, yet breathing out threatenings and slaughter against the disciples of the Lord, went unto the high priest, [2] And desired of him letters to Damascus to the synagogues, that if he found any of this way, whether they were men or women, he might bring them bound unto Jerusalem. [3] And as he journeyed, he came near Damascus: and suddenly there shined round about him a light from heaven: [4] and he fell to the earth and heard a voice saying unto him, Saul, Saul, why persecutest thou Me? [5] And he said, Who art thou, Lord? And the Lord said, I am Jesus whom thou persecutest: it is hard for thee to kick against the pricks."*
- Knocking for entrance at the heart's door
    1. *Revelation 3:20* *"Behold, I stand at the door, and knock: it any man hear my voice, and open the door, I will come in to him, and will sup with him, and he with Me."*

d. Commission
1. ***Revelation 1:11** "Saying, I am Alpha and Omega, the first and the last: and, What thou seest, write in a book, and send it unto the seven churches which are in Asia; unto Ephesus, and unto Smyrna, and unto Pergamos, and unto Thyatira, and unto Sardis, and unto Philadelphia, and unto Laodicea."*
2. The Command
   - ***Revelation 1:11** "What thou seest, write in a book"*
   - This does not simply mean those things which pertain to the seven churches, but he was to write the whole of the Revelation.
3. The Book
   - Just as there was a book of the generation of Adam **(Genesis 5:1)**, so there is to be a book of the last generations, both serving to anchor and guide all other generations.
   - The Book is the Bible. It was to be sent to the seven churches.

IX. TURNING TO GOD'S WORD – vs. 12
a. *"And I turned to see the voice that spake with me. And being turned, I saw seven golden candlesticks;" - vs. 12*
b. This is the voice of God
c. Christ is the Word
1. ***John 1:1-2** " [1] In the beginning was the Word, and the Word was with God, and the Word was God. [2] The same was in the beginning with God."*
d. We turn to the Word of God
1. In reverence
2. For redemption
3. For restoration
4. For rejoicing

X. THE GREAT AND TERRIBLE GOD – vs. 13-18

    a. **Revelation 13-18** *" [13] And in the midst of the seven candlesticks one like unto the Son of man, clothed with a garment down to the foot, and girt about the paps with a golden girdle. [14] His head and his hairs were white like wool, as white as snow; and His eyes were as a flame of fire; [15] And His feet like unto fine brass, as if they burned in a furnace; and His voice as the sound of many waters, [16] And He had in His right hand seven stars: and out of His mouth went a sharp twoedged sword: and His countenance was as the sun shineth in His strength. [17] And when I saw Him, I fell at His feet as dead. And He laid His right hand upon me, saying unto me, Fear not; I am the first and the last: [18] I am He that liveth, and was dead; and, behold, I am alive for evermore, Amen; and have the keys of hell and of death."*

    b. **Nehemiah 1:5** *"And said, I beseech thee, O Lord God of heaven, the great and terrible God, that keepeth covenant and mercy for them that love him and observe his commandments:"*

    c. The word "terrible" means to fear, to reverence, to be feared, it is that which is wonderful, which is astonishing, but which inspires devotion to God.

        1. **Proverbs 1:7(a)** *"The fear of the Lord is the beginning of knowledge:"*

    d. The great voice causes John to turn to see seven golden candlesticks. – **vs. 12**

        1. Priest and Judge – **vs. 13**
- The seven golden candlesticks are the seven churches.
- *"And in the mist of the seven golden candlesticks one like unto the Son of man,"*

  a. This is the glorified Christ
- The term *"Son of Man"* is used once more in **Revelation 14:14**. Jesus used this title frequently of Himself. It occurs eighty-four (84) times in the Gospels, twenty-one (21)

REVELATION—CHAPTER 1

of them being associated with His second coming.
- *"clothed with a garment down to the foot, and girt about the paps with a golden girdle."*
    a. His long garment speaks of His priestly character. As priest, He is not interceding, but judging just as the priest was to discern and judge in regard to leprosy **(Leviticus 13)**.

2. Penetration – **vs. 14**
    - *"His head and His hairs were white like wool, as white as snow; "*
        a. White hair in Scripture is symbolic of purity in character, dignity of age, authority as a Judge, and eternality.
    - *"and His eyes were as a flame of fire;"*
        a. His eyes as a flame of fire searches the mind, the heart, and the thoughts.

3. Place of Judgment – **vs. 15**
    - *"And His feet like unto fine brass, as if they burned in a furnace; and His voice as the sound of many waters,"*
        a. Brass indicates wrath; judgment of sin by the holiness of God
        b. His voice as the sound of many waters reveals the majesty and power and authority before whom all mankind must someday bow.

4. Position of Privilege – **vs. 16**
    - *"And He had in His right hand seven stars: and out of His mouth went a sharp twoedged sword: and His countenance was as the sun shineth in His strength."*
        a. In His right hand is the place of honor. The seven stars, which are explained in verse 20, are the angels of the seven churches.
        b. The word angel means messenger. I believe all of God's local assemblies have guardian angels.

EPISODES OF THE END, THE REVELATION OF JESUS CHRIST

      c. The word is also used for a human messenger which is the leader or Pastor.
- ***James 2:25** "Likewise also was not Rahab the harlot justified by works, when she had received the messengers, and had sent them out another way?"*
- ***Luke 9:52** "And sent messengers before his face: and they went, and entered into a village of the Samaritans, to make ready for him."*

5. Potentate Glory – **vs. 17-18**
- *[17] "And when I saw Him, I fell at His feet as dead. And He laid His right hand upon me, saying unto me, Fear not; I am the first and the last: [18] I am He that liveth, and was dead; and, behold, I am alive for evermore, Amen; and have the keys of hell and of death."*

      a. Potentate means ruler.
- ***I Timothy 6:15** "Which in His times He shall shew, who is the blessed and only Potentate, the King of kings, and Lord of lords;"*

      b. *"And when I saw Him, I fell at His feet as dead. And He laid His right hand upon me, saying unto me, Fear not; I am the first and the last:"* -

         1. John fell as if he were "dead"
- The fear of God has always prevailed in man's bosom. Whenever God has been pleased to reveal Himself, ever since the fall of Adam, the body in it's present weakness cannot endure the blaze of Divine Majesty.

         2. God's right hand upon John
- In tender compassion the Lord lays His right hand of

power upon John, bidding Him not to fear.
3. Assurance for John
- John is reassured by Christ's word concerning his person and nature. He is the Eternal One, He dominates time, He lived, lives and lives forever.
- He has supreme authority over death (the body), and hell (the soul).

XI. THE THREEFOLD COMMAND – vs. 19
   a.   What John saw in **Chapter 1**
       1.   ***"Write the things which thou hast seen, and the things which are, and the things which shall be hereafter;"***
- This verse is God's three-point outline for the entire book of Revelation.
  a. The Past
    - ***"Write the things which thou has seen,"*** **– Chapter 1**
  b. The Present
    - ***"and the things which are"*** **– Chapters 2 and 3**
  c. The Future
    - ***"and the things which shall be hereafter;"*** **– Chapters 4 through 22**

XII. THE INTERPRETATION OF WHAT HAD BEEN SEEN – vs. 20
   a.   ***"The mystery of the seven stars which thou sawest in My right hand, and the seven golden candlesticks. The seven stars are the angels of the seven churches: and the seven candlesticks which thou sawest are the seven churches."***
   b.   Verse 20 interprets what John had seen.

- c. As was pointed out in verse 16, the word angel means messenger and can refer to either an angelic being or a human being.
- d. In the Bible, stars represent angels.
  - *Job 38:7 "When the morning stars sang together, and all the sons of God shouted for joy?"*
  - *Isaiah 14:12 "How art thou fallen from heaven, O Lucifer, son of the morning! How art thou cut down to the ground, which didst weaken the nations!"*
- e. Angels are used by God to minister to His people
  - *Acts 7:53 "Who have received the law by the disposition of angels and have not kept it."*
  - *I Corinthians 4:9 "For I think that God hath set forth us the apostles last, as it were appointed to death: for we are made a spectacle unto the world, and to angels, and to men."*
  - *Hebrews 1:13-14 " [13] But to which of the angels said he at any time, Sit on my right hand, until I make thine enemies thy footstool? [14]] Are they not all ministering spirits, sent forth to minister for them who shall be heirs of salvation?"*
- f. Angels are appointed over nations
  - *Daniel 10:13 "But the prince of the kingdom of Persia withstood me one and twenty days: but, lo, Michael, one of the chief princes, came to help me; and I remained there with the kings of Persia."*
  - *Daniel 12:1 "And at that time shall Michael stand up, the great prince which standeth for the children of thy people: and there shall be a time of trouble, such as never was since there was a nation even to that same time: and at that time thy people shall be delivered, every one that shall be found written in the book."*
- g. God has Heavenly messengers and Human messengers. Both are known as angels. In **Revelation 1**, the angels there are human messengers who are the Pastors of the seven churches.

REVELATION—CHAPTER 1

Before we begin our study on the seven (07) Churches of Asia, let me give you a threefold view to consider.

I. We may look at them and describe what was actually true in these various assemblies at the time they were written. This is the historical view.

II. We may view them and apply them in a practical way to any assembly or individual at any period whose state might correspond with that described therein. This would be the practical view with lessons for ourselves from each Church.

III. We can consider them from the prophetic viewpoint as you see in the following outline.

CHURCH HISTORY PORTRAYED

Each letter to a specific Church describes characteristics of a particular period of Church history. We have the advantage now of looking back over these and can readily see how these various periods correspond with what is presented in these letters.

I. **Ephesus**
- Apostolic Period – AD 50-150

The word Ephesus means "desirable"; it indicates a virgin chosen by a young man to become his bride. And, so when Jesus left the Church in this world, she was as Paul says, a chaste virgin espoused to Christ **(II Corinthians 11:2)**. So, in chapter two (02) in the first seven (07) verses a description of the Apostolic Church.

II. **Smyrna**
- Roman Persecution Period – AD 150-300

The word Smyrna means "myrrh" which was an aromatic substance that exudes from a thorny tree and it had to be crushed in order to yield it's perfume and it's fragrance.

It is indeed a fitting name to describe the second period of the Church age, but soon after the Apostolic age came to a close, the persecutions of the Roman Empire fell upon the Church and the Church was literally like myrrh, ground into powder and scattered everywhere.

As for the ten (10) days, there were ten persecutions from Nero to Diocletian (AD 312). They were Nero, Domitian, Trajan, Antoninus, Severous, Maximian, Decius, Valerian, Aurelian, and Dioletian. Diocletian's persecution was the worst of all and lasted ten (10) years.

III. **Pergamos**
- Period AD 300-500

The word Pergamos means "marriage". In Pergamos there is quite a different state of things from that of the previous period given in Smyrna. There the Church was severely persecuted by ten (10) Roman Emperors for over one hundred (100) years. But, now with the victory of Constantine over Maxentious for the throne of the Roman Empire, the persecution against the Christians ceased.

Constantine claimed to have seen a vision of a flaming cross with the inscription, "By this Conquer". He then adopted the sign of the cross as the imperial standard of His armies and declared himself a convert to Christianity, though he was never baptized until near the end of his life. His conversion may be questioned. He saw the superiority of Christianity and the Christians were better citizens. Christians were given posts of honor and Bishops of the Church sat on thrones with the Nobles of the Empire. Constantine took his place now more openly to the whole world as head of the Church. But, at the same time, retained the office of the Pontifex Maximus, meaning the High Priest of the Heathen. This he never gave up.

Thus, the Church and state became allied. The Church and the world joined hands in an unholy marriage. Allegiance to Christ and His Word was sacrificed and the Lord had to say Pergamos was dwelling where Satan's seat was. In this way, pagans and Christians were united in an unholy alliance and pagan corruption, with a Christian name attached to it.

IV. Thyatira
- Period AD 500-1500

The word Thyatira means "never weary of sacrifice". Here we cover the period of history from approximately AD 500-1500, which is roughly one thousand (1000) years. Secular history cannot adequately explain why the dark ages came upon the world. You must know the Bible to understand that. Remember, it was at a time when the Church and the world were united. The Church had lost its power spiritually. And, now the Church, in the name of Jesus, began to put Jews and Christians to death if they would not join the Roman Church. This came from the Holy Roman Empire as it was called.

During this period, some Christians (little groups of them here and there like the Waldenses and Albigenses and others trying to hang on to the truth) were persecuted unmercifully by the Church at Rome. This is history. As you read the story of Jezebel in this chapter, you will have a description of the professing Church in the middle ages.

The darkness came because they had forsaken the Bible. They had forsaken the Lord and they began to set up a man made system in the name of Christ. If you want to know more about this, read Halley Handbook pages 765-783.

V. Sardis
- Period AD 1500-1900

The word Sardis means "remnant". Sardis represents the Protestant Reformation after the fire and devotedness to Christ and His Word cooled off. The reformation, which is definitely a work of God and also raised up such as Martin Luther (who was a Roman Catholic Monk) and others, began to examine the Scriptures and publicly proclaim what they found.

Luther found that wonder verse *"The just shall live by faith"* – **Galatians 3:11**. As a Roman Catholic Priest, he had beaten himself with a whip until he could hardly walk trying to atone for his sins, but found no relief. He found no rest for his soul. Then he found *"The just shall live by faith"* – **Galatians 3:11**; not by penance, not by beating oneself, not by climbing the sacred stairs in Rome, but by faith.

Sardis describes for us the rise and development, and finally the corruption of Protestantism. The reformation which was a powerful movement in its beginning did not maintain it's strong spiritual emphasis indefinitely.

VI. Philadelphia
- The Fundamental Church Period – A. D. 1750-1900

The word Philadelphia means "brotherly love". Philadelphia is the Church of the open door. A time of missionary expansion and world evangelism.

In 1792 William Carey, the father of the modern missionary movement, went to India, and in 1813 Adoniram Judson, went to Burman. There was powerful preaching by Whitfield, Wesley, Finney, Moody, Spurgeon, and a host of others. Was it not in the age of the open door when the humble Church with little strength took the saving message of Christ to the ends of the earth?

VII. Laodicea
- 'Till Christ Comes Period – AD 1850-present

The word Laodicea means "the people's rights". This is the professing Church in its last stage on earth before the Lord comes. It is so distasteful to the Lord that He spews it out of His mouth after calling for repentance. He is seen on the outside knocking for admittance. There is no improvement in the Church and this brings us to the end of "the things which are", perhaps from 1850, but certainly with us now.

Thyatira, Sardis, Philadelphia, Laodicea run concurrently until the Lord comes, after which Thyatira, Sardis, and Laodicea merge, and become part of Babylon the Great.

Revelation – Chapter 2

The Things Which Are: The Seven Churches

Ephesus – The Backslidden Church – Revelation 2:1-7

Ephesus means desirable. The Greeks used this term to describe the maiden of their choice. It indicates a virgin chosen by a young man to become his bride. And so, when Jesus left the Church in the world, she was as Paul says, a chaste virgin espoused unto Christ **(II Corinthians 11:2)**. The Church engaged to her risen Lord and glorified head. The marriage takes place in **Revelation 19:7-9**. The marriage of the Lamb is come and His wife hath made herself ready **(vs. 7)**. Ephesus established by Paul **(Acts 19)**. Ephesus had a great beginning. She had Paul, Timothy, and all truth **(Acts 20:20 and I Timothy 1:3)**.

I. **THE CONTROLLER** – vs. 1
   a. *"Unto the angel of the Church of Ephesus write; These things saith He that holdeth the seven stars in His right hand, who walketh in the midst of the seven golden candlesticks;"* – vs. 1
   b. Christ directed His letter to "the angel of the Church of Ephesus".
      1. The angel refers to a messenger or in today's terms, the Pastor, who with six other Pastors, was said to be in the Lord's "right hand" **(vs. 1)**.
- A symbol of God's authority and power.
      2. *"These things saith He that holdeth the seven stars in His right hand."* (vs. 1)
- When God holds the preacher in His right hand, He controls his
  - ❖ Ministry
  - ❖ Thoughts
  - ❖ Imagination
  - ❖ Body
  - ❖ Ways
  - ❖ Life

c. Christ walks in discrimination judgement among the seven Churches.
      1. **"Who walketh in the midst of the seven golden candlesticks." (vs.1)**

II. **THE COMMENDATION – vs. 2-3**
   a. For works and labor – **vs. 2**
      1. **"I know thy works and labor" (vs. 2)**
   b. For patience (steadfast) – **vs. 2**
   c. For stand against sin – **vs. 2**
      1. **"And how thou canst not bear them which are evil:" (vs. 2)**
   d. For loyalty to truth – **vs. 2**
      1. **"And though hast tried them which say they are apostles, and are not, and hast found them to be liars." (vs.2)**
   e. For concern as to Christ's name – **vs. 3**
      1. **"And hast borne, and hast patience, and for My Name's sake hast labored, and not fainted." (vs.3)**
   f. For hating Nicolaitanism – **vs. 6**

      1. The word Nicolaitanes means "conqueror of people". Apparently there were preachers and deacons who had attempted to rule or "conquer" the people of the Church.

III. **THE CHARGE – vs. 4**
   a. **"Nevertheless I have somewhat against thee, because thou hast left thy first love." – Revelation 2:4**
   b. They had left their first love
      1. **"Thou hast left thy first love" (vs. 4)**
      2. The Church in Ephesus was just as active as ever. It had not gone off into heresy, it had not fallen in shameful sin, it had not brought disgrace to the Name of Christ, but the Divine Spirit of Love had evaporated from the people's heart. Now their beautiful services were nothing but an empty show.

3. The Church needs
   - Tender Love
     - **Ephesians 4:32-33**
     - **Romans 12:10**
   - Total Love
     - **Matthew 22:37-40**
   - Devoted Love
     - **Revelation 12:11**
     - **II Chronicles 24:21**
     - **Mark 6:27**
     - **Luke 11:51**
     - **Acts 7:58**
     - **Acts 12:2**
     - **Hebrews 11:37**
   - Daily Love
     - **Acts 2:46**

IV. THE CALL TO REPENTANCE – vs. 5

a. *"Remember therefore from whence thou art fallen, and repent, and do the first works; or else I will come unto thee quickly, and will remove thy candlestick out of his place, except thou repent."* – Revelation 2:5

b. Remember
   1. *"Remember therefore from whence thou art fallen"* (vs. 5)
   2. This means that we are to remember how much we loved Him when we first met Him.
   3. Do you remember the agony of soul just prior to your accepting Christ as your Savior?
   4. Do you remember being brought face to face with your sin?
   5. Do you remember what blessed peace and joy that filled your soul when you saw the crucified One and He came into your life?
   6. This was the first love. Do you still have it?

c. Repent
   1. Having seen the gap between the life you are now living and the life you once lived, you must bridge through genuine repentance and return to your first love.

2. In any recovery, whether of an individual or a congregation, the memory of what has been lost often provides the first stirring of genuine repentance. "Repent" points to a crisis that takes the saints back to the point of departure. Repent means a "change of mind".
d. Repeat
1. ***"Do the first works" (vs. 5)***
2. First love is our affections to Christ
3. Set your affections on things above, not on things on the earth.
- **Colossians 3:2**

V. THE CAUTIOUS WARNING – vs. 5
a. *"... or else I will come unto thee quickly, and will remove thy candlestick out of his place, except thou repent."* – Revelation 2:5
b. When God removes the candlestick
1. Power is gone
2. Peace is gone
3. Prosperity is gone

We have already looked at verse 6 under the heading "Commendation". We will have more on verse 6 when we get to verses 14 and 15.

VI. THE CONCLUSION – vs. 7
a. *"He that hath an ear, let him hear what the Spirit saith unto the Churches; to Him that overcometh will I give to eat of the tree of life, which is in the mist of the paradise of God."* – Revelation 2:7
b. The call to the hearing ear
1. *"He that hath an ear, let him hear what the Spirit saith unto the Churches;"* (vs. 7)
2. To the individual who has an ear to hear, the appeal is made to listen and to heed what the Spirit saith to the Churches.
3. This appeal would indicate that every believer that is here is made responsible to understand

REVELATION—CHAPTER 2

               the state of things around him in the professing Church.
- 4. The whole Church is addressed by the call to hear, but only the exercised individual with an open ear will respond to it.

  c. The promise to the overcomer
- 1. ***"... to Him that overcometh will I give to eat of the tree of life, which is in the mist of the paradise of God."* (vs. 7)**
- 2. Adam lost the right to eat of the tree of life in the garden of Eden when he sinned and was driven out.
- 3. The overcomer is promised the tree of life in the paradise of God which will never be lost.

Smyrna – The Persecuted Church – Revelation 2:8-11

I. THE CRUSHING – vs. 8

  a. The word Smyrna means Myrrh (Myrrh meaning bitter). It was a gum resin taken from a shrubbery bush by crushing it.

  b. Myrrh was used in:
- 1. Making perfume – **Psalm 45:8**
- 2. Anointing oil for the Priests – **Exodus 30:23-30**
- 3. Purification of women – **Esther 2:12**
- 4. Embalming – **John 19:39**

  c. The Church was in
- 1. Bitterness of trial
- 2. Sorrow
- 3. Death
- 4. Suffering

  d. ***"...the first and the last..."* – vs. 8**
- 1. Creation and redemption began with Him.
- 2. Eternal damnation or salvation, loss or gain, punishment or glory, are all depending on what we do with Christ.
  - Two Characteristics of the Church in the first three centuries
    - 1. Material poverty
    - 2. Spiritual power

- Two Characteristics of the Church in the twenty-first century
  1. Material wealth
  2. Spiritual weakness

e. *"... Fear not; I am the first and the last: I am He that liveth, and was dead; and, behold, I am alive for evermore, Amen; ..."* – Revelation 1:17(b) – 1:18(a)

II. THE CRISIS – vs. 9
a. The Lord in wonderful grace encourages and commends this tried Church.
  1. *"I know thy works"* (vs. 9)
     - Their works were wrought in the fiery furnace of afflictions and trials, and God was pleased with their works.
  2. *"and tribulation"* (vs. 9)
     - *"We glory in tribulation, also knowing that tribulation worketh patience."* – Romans 5:3
  3. *"and poverty"* (vs. 9)
     - The material poverty of Smyrna was great, but the Lord in His commendation said, *"but thou art rich"*.
  4. *"and I know the blasphemy of them which say they are Jews, and are not, but are the synagogue of Satan."* (vs. 9)
     - These people were Jews by birth, but not by faith. They were motivated by Satan to persecute and slander the Church. The word "synagogue" means "a gathering together" which is in contrast to the "church" which means "a gathering out". One settles in the world, and the other is gathered out of the world.
     - Down through the ages, Satan has tried to destroy the Church. He may kill the messenger, but not the message. Jesus said, *"...and upon this rock I will build my Church; and the gates of hell shall not prevail against it."* – Matthew 16:18

III. THE CONTINUED HATRED OF SATAN AGAINST THE CHURCH – vs. 10

    a.   The Lord encourages them to have no fear of their sufferings, of their imprisonment by the devil, or whatever else may come.

    b.   He limits the tribulation to ten (10) days.
- Ten (10) speaks of responsibility (i.e. the ten commandments). This indicates that their suffering would not go beyond what they could bear, though these afflictions would be severe.

    c.   Comfort
        1.   *"... be thou faithful unto death..."* (vs. 10)
- *"... Well done, thou good and faithful servant: thou hast been faithful over a few things, I will make thee ruler over many things: enter thou into the joy of thy lord."* – **Matthew 25:21**

    d.   Crown
        1.   *"... and I will give thee a crown of life."* (vs. 10)
- This is the martyr's crown

IV. THE CHURCHES – vs. 11

    a.   The readers are challenged to take the message to heart.
- *"He that hath an ear, let him hear what the Spirit saith unto the Churches:"* (vs. 11)

    b.   The Promise
        1.   *" ... He that overcometh shall not be hurt of the second death."* (vs. 11)
        2.   *"For whatsoever is born of God overcometh the world: and this is the victory that overcometh the world, even our faith."* – **I John 5:4**
        3.   No believer will ever suffer the second death.

EPISODES OF THE END, THE REVELATION OF JESUS CHRIST

> Pergamos – The Compromising Church - Revelation 2:12-17

I. **THE MARRIAGE** – vs. 12-13
- a. *"[12] And to the angel of the church in Pergamos write; These things saith he which hath the sharp sword with two edges; [13] I know thy works, and where thou dwellest, even where Satan's seat is: and thou holdest fast my Name, and hast not denied my faith, even in those days wherein Antipas was my faithful martyr, who was slain among you, where Satan dwelleth."* Revelation 2:12-13
- b. The word Pergamos means marriage. When the devil finds out that he can't destroy anything he has attacked, then he seeks to join it and destroy it from within.
- c. The devil succeeded in leading the church at Ephesus away from their first love **(Revelation 2:4)**. At Smyrna he led a great persecution against the church. When the devil found out he could not destroy the church, he decided to join the church. This is exactly what he did at Pergamos and the church and the state were joined together.
- d. When the Church yokes up with the world, she loses:
  - Her pilgrimage
  - Her power
  - Her peace
  - Her purity
  1. Penetration Judgement – **vs. 12**
     - a. *"... These things saith he which hath the sharp sword with two edges."* (vs. 12)
     - b. Piercing our works and the motive behind our works
  2. Satan's seat (throne) in the city of Pergamos – **vs. 13**
     - a. *"...I know thy works, and where thou dwellest, even where Satan's seat is:..."* (vs. 13)

REVELATION—CHAPTER 2

        b.   God commended their works in the midst of such evil **(vs. 13)**.
        c.   Satan's seat (throne) was moved into the city of Pergamos.
        d.   Satan's throne is not in hell. He is the prince of this world. – **John 12:31**

3. They were holding fast His Name – **vs. 13**
    a.   ***"...thou holdest fast My Name,..."*** **(vs. 13)**
    b.   They did not deny His Name.
    c.   They were loyal to God in the shadow of Satan's throne.

4. They had not denied His faith – **vs. 13**
    a.   ***"... and hast not denied my faith,..."*** **(vs. 13)**
    b.   They did not deny His faith.

5. Christ recognized Antipas, referring to him as my faithful martyr.
    a.   Antipas means "against all".
    b.   He died standing faithful to the Name and doctrine of Christ.
    c.   Nothing is known about Antipas by men, but God knows.
    d.   In verse 13 we have:
- Martyrdom
    - ❖ Antipas, My faithful martyr
- Marked
    - ❖ "Holdest fast My name". We are marked by the name "Christian".
- Madness
    - ❖ "Antipas, who was slain among you".

II.   THE MIXING – vs. 14-15

    a.   ***" [14] But I have a few things against thee, because thou hast there them that hold the doctrine of Balaam, who taught Balac to cast a stumbling block before the children of Israel, to eat things sacrificed unto idols, and to commit fornication. [15] So hast thou also them that hold*** *the doctrine of the Nicolaitanes, which thing I hate."* – **Revelation 2:14-15**

b. Doctrine of Balaam was teaching Balac to corrupt the people who could not be cursed **(Numbers 31:15-16; 22:5; and 23:8)**. By tempting them to marry the women of Moab, they lost their separation. When Satan could not physically destroy the Israelites, he tried to destroy them with ungodly neighbors so that Israel would no longer be separated for the Lord but be defiled with idolatrous and immoral practices.

I quote from F. A. Tatford's commentary on Revelation:

"Balaam's teaching was therefore in complete conformity with the libertinism of those who taught that conversion to Christianity left the individual free to live as he pleased and that attendance at heathen festivals, engaging in pagan worship, and participation in religious prostitution were not practices for which a Christian should be condemned.

Two temptations constantly confronted the Gentile believers in the early days of the Church.

I. THE EATING OF IDOL MEAT

When the problem arose at Corinth, Paul advised the Christians not to inquire whether food which they purchased or which was set before them at a meal had been presented to an idol, but to eat without question. If however, another person stated that the meat has been presented to an idol, they should refrain from eating it in order not to stumble others **(I Corinthians 10:25-29)**. *Even today, the child of God finds the need at time to sacrifice legitimate pleasure of activities as an indication of his allegiance to Christ.*

II. FORNICATION

Within the precincts of every temple, harlot priestesses offered themselves for prostitution as part of their service to the god or goddess worshipped.

The Lord held this against the Church at Pergamos that some tolerated the impure practices in which they had previously indulged and suffered with protest (even if they did not actually encourage) the leading astray of God's people. Today moral standards are fast slipping, even among the Church. We are told that nothing can of itself always be labeled wrong." – end of quote from F. A. Tatford's commentary on Revelation.

    c.   What was in Ephesus was "deeds" **(Rev. 2:6)**, had in Pergamos become a doctrine **(Rev. 2:15)**.

    d.   Nicolaitanism is a sinful attempt of man, or man-made religious systems, to usurp power over the Church. The power belongs exclusively to Christ. He is the head of the Church **(Ephesians 1:22)**.

III. THE MOVING – vs. 16

a. **"Repent; or else I will come unto thee quickly, and will fight against them with the sword of my mouth." – Revelation 2:16**

b. The exhortation consists of one word, repent. There must be a change or the Lord Jesus Christ will smite with the Sword of His mouth.

    1.   **" [12] For the Word of God is quick and powerful, and sharper than any twoedged sword piercing even to the dividing asunder of soul and spirit, and of the joints and marrow, and is a discerner of the thoughts and intents of the heart. [13] Neither is there any creature that is no manifest in his sight: but all things are naked and opened unto the eyes of him with whom we have to do." – Hebrews 4:12-13**

    2.   When God's judgement moves against people, the consequences are terrible.
- People in Noah's day – **Genesis 6 and 7**
- Korah – **Numbers 16**
- Achan – **Joshua 7**
- Ananias and Sapphira – **Acts 5**

    3.   God is not a person to be trifled with. Do not treat Him lightly.

IV. **THE MANNA** – vs. 17
- a. *"He that hath an ear, let him hear what the Spirit saith unto the Churches: To him that overcometh will I give to eat of the hidden manna, and will give him a white stone, and in the stone a new name written which no man knoweth saving he that receiveth it."* – **Revelation 2:17**
- b. The overcomer's future reward is to eat of the hidden manna, which is a type of the Word of God.
- c. To those willing to separate themselves from this wicked world, they will feast on bread from heaven.
    1. Jesus said, *"...I am the bread of life..."* – **John 6:31-35**
- e. Judicial interpretation of stones
    1. Juries made their decisions by casting a white stone for acquittal or a black stone if guilty.
- f. Spiritual interpretation of the white stone
    1. A white stone used in numbers and calculation shows that we are among the children of God.
    2. The Christian does not receive the black stone of condemnation, but receives the white stone of salvation through the merits of Jesus, who died for the sinners.
    3. A white stone was known as a "victory" stone to the ancients.
        - *"But thanks be to God, which giveth us the victory through our Lord Jesus Christ."* – **I Corinthians 15:57**

Thyatira – The Church Settled in Sin – Revelation 2:18-29

I. THE SACRIFICE – vs. 18
    a. *"And unto the angel of the Church in Thyatira write; These things saith the Son of God, who hath His eyes like unto a flame of fire, and His feet are like fine brass;"* – **Revelation 2:18**
    b. Thyatira means "never weary of sacrifice". It suggests continuous, public, formal, and shallow ritualism.

II. THE SON – vs. 18
    a. The eyes of fire read the inner motives and pierce the ritualistic shams of man. God's discerning demands spiritual reality.
        1. *"The Lord is in His holy temple, the Lord's throne is in heaven: His eyes behold, His eyelids try the children of men."* – **Psalm 11:4**
        2. *"He ruleth by His power for ever; His eyes behold the nations: Let not the rebellious exalt themselves. Selah."* – **Psalm 66:7**
        3. *"The eyes of the Lord are in every place, beholding the evil and the good."* – **Proverbs 15:3**
    b. The Lord's discerning eyes try the righteous and the wicked, approving the one, and rejecting the other.

III. THE SERVICE – vs. 19
    a. *"I know thy works, and charity, and service, and faith, and thy patience, and thy works; and the last to be more than the first."* – **Revelation 2:19**
    b. God commended them for increasing service.
        1. However, they stood for some things, but did not stand against anything.
    c. They were rich in social service.
        2. This is fine, but is second to reaching the unsaved.

      d.   The last works were more than the first works.
      3.   A big report is not always a sign of a spiritual Church.

IV. THE SUFFEREST – vs. 20
    a.   ***"Notwithstanding, I have a few things against thee, because thou sufferest that woman Jezebel which calleth herself a prophetess, to teach and to seduce my servants to commit fornication, and to eat things sacrificed unto idols."*** **– Revelation 2:20**
    b.   The word sufferest means "to allow".
        1.   They tolerated sin and failed to judge sin.

V. THE SEDUCER – vs. 20
    a.   There were some individuals, particularly women, who were the chief cause of the troubled in the Church at Thyatira, which resulted in the strong rebuke from the Lord.
    b.   The teaching of these Jezebels had corrupted God's people like the Jezebel of old.
        1.   Jezebel was a Phoenician princess who, after marrying King Ahab, brought Baal worship to Israel **(I Kings 16:28-34)**.
        2.   This self-proclaimed prophetess counseled Christians within the Church to become involved in Roman religious practices of "fornication, and to eat things sacrificed unto idols".
        3.   Jezebel was out of her place, never called of God, and misleading the people.

VI. THE SPACE – vs. 21
    a.   ***"And I gave her a space to repent of her fornication; and she repented not."*** **– Revelation 2:21**
    b.   God patiently waited for repentance to come, but the woman declined.

REVELATION—CHAPTER 2

    c.   *"...God waited in the days of Noah, while the ark was a preparing wherein few, that is, eight souls were saved..."* – I Peter 3:20

    d.   No word is found where the literal Jezebel of the Old Testament ever repented. Her last act was to paint her face and attempt to conceal her identity **(II Kings 9:30)**. Of this Jezebel system, the risen Lord says, *"she repented not"*.

VII. THE SORROW – vs. 22-23

    a.   *" [22] Behold, I will cast her into a bed, and them that commit adultery with her into great tribulation, except they repent of their deeds. [23] And I will kill her children with death; and all the Churches shall know that I am he which searcheth the reins and hearts: and I will give unto every one of you according to your works."* – Revelation 2:22-23

    b.   Those who follow Jezebel's teachings will be left behind at the rapture.

    c.   God brought three (03) judgements upon her and her followers:

        1.   He would *"cast her into a bed"*. **(vs. 22)**
- From a bed of immorality into a sick bed of disease and, in the end, death.

        2.   *"...and them who commit adultery with her, into great tribulation except they repent of their deeds."* **(vs. 22)**
- Repent or perish

        3.   *"And I will kill her children with death..."* **(vs. 23)**
- All of her followers, both original followers and a second generation of professing believers, would suffer the same fate.
- Their doom left no doubt for the Church that this judgement was from God.
  - ❖ *"and all the Churches shall know that I am he which searcheth the reins and hearts..."* **(vs. 23)**

- ❖ Reins means "kidneys" and in the Bible this denotes the inward affections.
- ❖ Hearts speaks of the thoughts that motivate the will from which actions spring.
- ❖ *"...and I will give unto every one of your according to your works."* (vs. 23)

    d. God will judge every Church. We must keep it simple:
        1. Preach the Word
        2. Pray
        3. Teach the Word
        4. Sing
        5. Witness

VIII. SATAN – vs. 24

    a. *"But unto you I say, and unto the rest in Thyatira, as many as have not this doctrine, and which have not known the depths of Satan, as they speak; I will put upon you none other burden."* – Revelation 2:24

    b. Not all had yielded to Jezebel's doctrine. There was a godly remnant who did not follow the corruption of the Church, but rather denounced its unbiblical ways.

    c. *"...the depths of Satan..."* is a complete abandonment to evil. The Lord in compassion would lay no other burden on them; they were suffering much for the truth.

IX. THE SECOND COMING – vs. 25

    a. *"But that which ye have already hold fast till I come."* – Revelation 2:25

    b. They were not able to stem the tide of Jezebel's doctrine. God told them to hold fast to what they had until He comes.

    c. How easy it is to leave our first love in apostate surroundings.

X. THE SHIFT – vs. 26-27

a. *"[26] And he that overcometh, and keepeth My works unto the end, to him will I give power over the nations: [27] And he shall rule them with a rod of iron; as the vessels of a potter shall they be broken to shivers: even as I received of my Father." –* Revelation 2:26-27

b. There will be a shift of power from man to God. Overcomers will share in Christ's power and rule over the nations. This refers to **Psalm 2:8-9** in which God backs by an oath, His solemn promise, that His Son the Messiah, will rule the nations. Christ will share this promise with the Church **(Romans 8:17)**. This is the first definite view of the millennial in Revelation.

XI. THE STAR – vs. 28

a. *"And I will give him the morning star." –* Revelation 2:28

b. This promise is to all who are His. The gift is Christ Himself.

    1. *"I am the root and offspring of David, and the bright and morning star." –* **Revelation 22:16**

c. While we wait for that glorious day, the Church must occupy until He comes **(Luke 19:13)**.

d. We, like the saints at Thyatira, must fight to keep the Lord's works to the end and defend *"the faith which was once delivered unto the saints"* **(Jude vs. 3)**.

XII. THE SPIRIT'S SAYING – vs. 29

a. *"He that hath an ear, let him hear what the Spirit saith unto the Churches." –* Revelation 2:29

b. Christ closed His letter to Thyatira as He did the other Churches.

c. To "hear" means to "heed"; to "heed" means to "act"; to "act" means to be *"doers of the Word, and not hearers only."* **(James 1:22)**

Revelation – Chapter 3

Sardis – The Dead Church – Revelation 3:1-6

I. **THE ESCAPING ONES** – vs. 1
    a. *"AND unto the angel of the church in Sardis write; These things saith he that hath the seven Spirits of God, and the seven stars; I know thy works, that thou hast a name that thou livest, and art dead."* – **Revelation 3:1**
    b. Sardis means "the escaping ones".
        1. What a fitting name for saved individuals at any time.
        2. Those who have trusted Christ's work on Calvary have been delivered from:
- Sin
- Evil world
- Hell
- Second death

II. **THE ENTOMBED** – vs. 1
    a. *"... thou hast a name that thou livest, and art dead."* (vs. 1)
    b. They had a name, they were alive, but they were dead.
        1. Many Churches would be right at home in a graveyard.
        2. Many Church members have never been born again.

III. **THE ESTABLISHING** – vs. 2
    a. *"Be watchful, and strengthen the things which remain, that are ready to die: for I have not found thy works perfect before God."* – Revelation 3:2
        1. *"...I have not found thy works perfect before God"* suggests having been

sidetracked from the purpose and work God had called them to do.
            2. If we don't watch, Satan will sidetrack us and wreck our lives.
        b. Twice as a city, Sardis had been conquered because she failed to watch.
        c. The word *"strengthen"* means
            1. To fix
            2. Make fast
            3. To set
            4. Establish

IV. **THE EXHORTATION** – vs. 3
   a. *"Remember therefore how thou hast received and heard, and hold fast, and repent. If therefore thou shalt not watch, I will come on thee as a thief, and thou shalt not know what hour I will come upon thee."* – Revelation 3:3
   b. They were to remember the truth and blessings they had received.
   c. God pleads for correction of errors in departing from them. Such a correction will produce a returning to them and holding them.
   d. God says to remember, repent, and hold fast; if not, He says *"I will come on thee as a thief, and thou shalt not know what hour I will come upon thee."* (vs. 3)
   e. God will come in judgement and judge the Church.

V. **THE EVIDENCE** – vs. 4
   a. *"Thou hast a few names even in Sardis which have not defiled their garments; and they shall walk with me in white: for they are worthy."* – Revelation 3:4
   b. A few had not defiled their garments.
   c. God always has His witnesses in every age. Their lives are evidences of the new birth.

VI. THE ENCOURAGEMENT – vs. 4
    a.   *"...and they shall walk with me in white: for they are worthy." – Revelation 3:4*
    b.   By accepting Christ as their righteousness, they were made worthy before God.
        1.   **Romans 10:4**
        2.   **II Corinthians 5:21**
        3.   **Ephesians 1:6**
    c.   He encourages them by assurance that they will walk with Him in white.

VII. THE EXEMPTION – vs. 5
    a.   *"He that overcometh, the same shall be clothed in white raiment; and I will not blot out his name out of the book of life, but I will confess his name before My Father, and before His angels." – Revelation 3:5*
    b.   Who are the overcomers?
        1.   *"For whatsoever is born of God overcometh the world: and this is the victory that overcometh the world, even our faith. Who is he that overcometh the world, but he that believeth that Jesus is the Son of God?" – I John 5:4-5*
        2.   The Roman Church thinks it can blot a person's name out of the Book of Life.
- The Lord says *"... I will not blot out his name of the book of life, but I will confess his name before My Father, and before His angels." – Revelation 3:5*
- *"Whosoever therefore shall confess Me before men, him will I confess also before My Father which is in heaven." – Matthew 10:32*

        3.   There are two Books:
- The Book of Life
    - ❖ The Book of Life is the record of all who have ever lived, whether inside or outside the womb of the mother.

- ❖ When a person rejects Jesus Christ as their personal Savior and dies in their sin, their name is then removed from the Book of Life.
- ❖ They will suffer the second death and will stand before the Great White Throne Judgement which is for unbelievers.
- The Lamb's Book of Life
  - ❖ The Lamb's Book of Life is the record of all who have trusted and accepted the Lord Jesus Christ as their personal Savior.
  - ❖ No name can be blotted out of the Lamb's Book of Life because salvation is eternal.
    - ♦ *" [28] And I give unto them eternal life; and they shall never perish, neither shall any man pluck them out of My Hand. [29] My Father, which gave them Me, is greater than all; and no man is able to pluck them out of My Father's hand."* – John 10:28-29

VIII. THE ENDING EXHORTATION – vs. 6
   a. *"He that hath an ear, let him hear what the Spirit saith unto the churches."* – Revelation 3:6
   b. A spiritual ear can only be received through spiritual regeneration. Such hearing means:
      1. Heeding
      2. Doing
      3. Obedience

Philadelphia – The Fundamental Church – Revelation 3:7-13

Philadelphia means "brotherly love". This was the fundamental Church.

I. **BROTHERLY LOVE – vs. 7**
    a. **"And to the angel of the church in Philadelphia write; These things saith He that is holy, He that is true, He that hath the key of David, He that openeth, and no man shutteth; and shutteth, and no man openeth;"** – Revelation 3:7
    b. These should be the characteristics of all the assemblies of God's people.
        1. **"Be kindly affectioned one to another with brotherly love; in honour preferring one another;"** – Romans 12:10
        2. **"Let brotherly love continue."** – Hebrews 13:1
        3. **"But if ye bite and devour one another, take heed that ye be not consumed one of another."** – Galatians 5:15
        4. We are to honor one another with God honoring love.
          • I Corinthians 13:1-8
    c. Christ presents Himself in three ways to Philadelphia
        1. *"...He that is holy,..."* (vs. 7)
          • Right in character
          • Jesus Christ, as God, is holy and entirely set apart and separated from sin and sinners.
        2. *"...He that is true,..."* (vs. 7)
          • Right in conduct
          • Christ is the one true God, distinct from all others.
          • What He says is truth
            ❖ **"Jesus saith unto him, I am the way, the truth, and the life; no man cometh unto the Father, but by Me."** – John 14:6
        3. *"...He that hath the key of David,..."* (vs. 7)
          • Right in authority

- The key of David is mentioned in **Isaiah 22:20-22**. King Hezekiah's treasurer, Shebna, abused and misused the authority of his office. – **Isaiah 22:15-25**
- Eliakim, who was a type of Christ, replaced Shebna. He was given authority over the King's treasury.
- Both Jesus and Eliakim have authority to bind or loose which no one has the right to alter. Jesus' authority is absolute. However, Eliakim's authority is subject to the King.

II. <u>BOLDNESS</u> – vs. 8

a. *"I know thy works: behold, I have set before thee an open door, and no man can shut it: for thou hast a little strength, and hast kept My word, and hast not denied My name."* – **Revelation 3:8**

b. God opened doors and shut doors for the Apostles in the early days of the Church.
- **Acts 16:6-10**
- **Acts 18:9-10**
- *"For a great door and effectual is opened unto me, and there are many adversaries."* – **I Corinthians 16:9**

c. *"But Esaias is very bold, and saith, I was found of them that sought me not; I was made manifest unto them that asked not after me."* – **Romans 10:20**
   1. God opens or shuts the door of Heaven.
      - He knows those who are worthy to enter
   2. God opens or shuts the door of Divine truth.
      - He opens to the honest seekers
   3. God opens or shuts the door of service. – **Acts 16:6-7**
      - The temptation is to force open a door. Wisdom says to wait.

d. The reasons why God kept the door open:
   1. They had a little strength.
   2. They had kept the Word of God.

3. They had not denied His Name.
   - The reason that the doors of service and spiritual power have been closed to many Churches today, is because they do not believe the Bible is the Word of God, therefore, they are denying His Name.
   - Numerically, Philadelphia was not very strong. But, God had infused this faithful group with spiritual power enabling them to be true to His Name and His Word in the midst of satanic opposition.
   - Effective service does not depend upon the size of a Church, but upon its availability to be used.

III. BOWING – vs. 9
    a. *"Behold, I will make them of the synagogue of Satan, which say they are Jews, and are not, but do lie; behold, I will make them to come and worship before thy feet, and to know that I have loved thee."* **– Revelation 3:9**
    b. We may not live long enough to see our enemies bow at our feet, but God will see to it in His time.
    c. The time is coming when every knee will bow.
        1. *"For it is written, As I live, saith the Lord, every knee shall bow to Me, and every tongue shall confess to God.* **– Romans 14:11**

IV. BEAUTIFUL PROMISE – vs. 10
    a. *"Because thou hast kept the word of My patience, I also will keep thee from the hour of temptation, which shall come upon all the world, to try them that dwell upon the earth."* **– Revelation 3:10**
    b. What is this hour of temptation?
        1. This is the tribulation period **(Revelation chapters 6 through 19)** that is to come upon the whole world to try them that dwell upon the earth.

2. It is the time of God's wrath upon this earth. Read **Daniel 11:36-12:1; Matthew 24:15-22**; and **Revelation chapters 6 through 19**. This is the seventieth week of Daniel, which is seven years. We will study the seventieth week of Daniel a little later.
- c. Will the Church go through the tribulation?
    1. *"Because thou hast kept the word of My patience, I also will keep thee from the hour of temptation,..."* (vs. 10)
    2. The word "temptation" refers to the "tribulation".
    3. The believer is saved from the wrath to come. This is God's sure word.
        - *"And to wait for His Son from heaven, whom He raised from the dead, even Jesus, which delivered us from the wrath to come."* – I Thessalonians 1:10
        - *"For God hath not appointed us to wrath, but to obtain salvation by our Lord Jesus Christ."* – I Thessalonians 5:9
    4. We notice two "keeps" in **Revelation 3:10**
        - *"...thou hast kept the word of My patience..."*
        - *"...I also will keep thee from the hour of temptation..."*
        - They kept His word, now He will keep them from the hour of tribulation.
        - He will catch away the Church to be with Him in heaven before the tribulation begins.
            ❖ I Thessalonians 4:13-18
            ❖ Revelation 4:1

V. BURDEN OF THE BOOK – vs. 11
- a. *"Behold, I come quickly: hold that fast which thou hast, that no man take thy crown."* – Revelation 3:11
- b. They were to hold fast to the truth already received, and to hold ground that they already possessed (*"...that no man take thy crown."* or reward).

EPISODES OF THE END, THE REVELATION OF JESUS CHRIST

VI. **BRIDES HOME** – vs. 12
- a. *"Him that overcometh will I make a pillar in the temple of my God, and he shall go no more out: and I will write upon him the name of my God, and the name of the city of my God, which is new Jerusalem, which cometh down out of heaven from my God: and I will write upon him my new name."* – Revelation 3:12
- b. The bride's home is "new Jerusalem".
- c. The Philadelphia letter assures that overcomers will be made pillars in the temple of God. In apostolic days, pillars were erected to rulers and generals with testimonies of their accomplishments chiseled upon them.
- d. In glory, the overcomer will be a permanent testimony to victories through Christ's grace.
- e. The believer will have three names.
  1. He will have the name of "my God".
     - This name emphasizes God's "ownership" of the believer.
  2. He will have the name of the "city of my God".
     - This name emphasizes his citizenship in the heavenly city.
  3. He will have written on him "my new name".
     - This emphasizes his universal role before God. My new name describes Christ's fullness and glory. This fullness and glory will never be known until saved ones experience it when they see Christ and become like Him.
       - ❖ *"Beloved, now are we the sons of God, and it doth not yet appear what we shall be: but we know that, when He shall appear, we shall be like Him; for we shall see Him as He is."* – I John 3:2

VII. **BENEDICTION** – vs. 13
- a. *"He that hath an ear, let him hear what the Spirit saith unto the churches."* Revelation 3:13

> b. The Holy Spirit keeps speaking to all open ears and willing hearts in these solemn messages. Are we listening?
>
> c.

Laodicea – The Church that Christ Spews Out
Revelation 3:14-22

I. <u>LAODICEA</u> – vs. 14
a. ***"And unto the angel of the church of the Laodiceans write; These things saith the Amen, the faithful and true witness, the beginning of the creation of God;"* – Revelation 3:14**
b. Laodicea means "the people's rights".
c. The people themselves had taken over the Church and the Lord was no longer the head of the Church.
d. They wanted a preacher who would tickle their ears.
  1. ***"For the time will come when they will not endure sound doctrine; but after their own lusts shall they heap to themselves teachers, having itching ears;"* – II Timothy 4:3**
e. Three titles of our Lord
  1. *"...the Amen..."* – means truth **(vs. 14)**
     - Christ is the final truth. Beyond Him, God has nothing more to say to man.
     - ***"Beloved, when I gave all diligence to write unto you of the common salvation, it was needful for me to write unto you, and exhort you that ye should earnestly contend for the faith which was once delivered unto the saints."* – Jude 3**
  2. *"...the faithful and true witness..."* **(vs. 14)**
     - Everything He says is true and you can depend upon it.
  3. *"...the beginning of the creation of God..."* **(vs. 14)**
     - This does not teach that Jesus is the first of God's creation. But, rather, it teaches that creation had its beginning in Him.

- ❖ *"I am Alpha and Omega, the beginning and the ending, saith the Lord, which is, and which was, and which is to come, the Almighty."* – **Revelation 1:8**
- ❖ *"All things were made by Him, and without Him was not any thing made that was made."* – **John 1:3**
- ❖ *"For by Him were all things created, that are in heaven, and that are in earth, visible and invisible, whether they be thrones, or dominions, or principalities, or powers: all things were created by Him, and for Him:"* – **Colossians 1:16**

II. <u>LUKEWARM</u> – vs. 15-16

    a.   *" [15] I know thy works, that thou art neither cold nor hot: I would thou wert cold or hot. [16] So then because thou art lukewarm, and neither cold nor hot, I will spue thee out of my mouth."* – **Revelation 3:15-16**

    b.   Lukewarm water is nauseating.

    c.   God says, you make Me sick.

        1.   *"A double minded man is unstable in all his ways."* – **James 1:8**

        2.   *"And Elijah came unto all the people, and said, How long halt ye between two opinions?..."* – **I Kings 18:21**

        3.   Undecided, neutral positions toward God and truth are so hateful and sickening; they must be gotten rid of at once.

III. <u>LUXURY</u> – vs. 17

    a.   *"Because thou sayest, I am rich, and increased with goods, and have need of nothing; and knowest not that thou art wretched, and miserable, and poor, and blind, and naked:"* – **Revelation 3:17**

    b.   The present day Church is rich and increased with goods. We are rich in material things but minus in heavenly treasures.
        1.   ***" [19] Lay not up for yourselves treasures upon earth, where moth and rust doth corrupt, and where thieves break through and steal: [20] But lay up for yourselves treasures in heaven, where neither moth nor rust doth corrupt, and where thieves do not break through nor steal: [21] For where your treasure is, there will your heart be also."* – Matthew 6:19-21**
        2.   The Church concentrates on man rather than Christ. It is occupied with the temporal rather than the spiritual.
        3.   It is:
- Self-centered
- Self-occupied
- Self-satisfied
- Self-sufficient
- Over confident
- Proud
- Boastful

IV.   LOSS OF POWER – vs. 17
    a.   *"...and knowest not that thou are wretched, and miserable, and poor, and blind, and naked:"* – **Revelation 3:17**
    b.   Their ignorance was they did not know their true condition.
    c.   Like Samson, ***"He wist not that the Lord had departed from him."* – Judges 16:20-21**
    d.   Samson's strength was restored but his vision was not.
    e.   The Church never fully recovered from the stroke at Ephesus
        1.   Left their first love – **Revelation 2:4**

V.   LOW STANDARDS – vs. 17

    a.   **"Because thou sayest, I am rich, and increased with goods, and have need of nothing; and knowest not that thou art wretched, and miserable, and poor, and blind, and naked:"** – Revelation 3:17
    b.   In the average Church, the Bible is not the standard any more.
    c.   It has been kicked out of the
        1.   Church
        2.   Schools
        3.   Homes
        4.   Hearts

VI.   LOOSE LIVING – vs. 17
    a.   **"Because thou sayest, I am rich, and increased with goods, and have need of nothing; and knowest not that thou art wretched, and miserable, and poor, and blind, and naked:"** – Revelation 3:17
    b.   Today we have preachers, deacons, and Church laymen who are
        1.   Drinking
        2.   Lying
        3.   Cursing
        4.   Cheating
        5.   Dressing immodestly
        6.   Committing adultery
    c.   May the Lord have mercy on us and help us all.

VII.   LACK OF CLOTHING – vs. 17
    d.   **"... that thou art wretched, and miserable, and poor, and blind, and naked:"** – Revelation 3:17
    e.   Material riches of Laodicea could not cover their moral nakedness.

REVELATION—CHAPTER 3

VIII.　LOVING COUNSEL – vs. 18-19
    a.　*"[18] I counsel thee to buy of me gold tried in the fire, that thou mayest be rich; and white raiment, that thou mayest be clothed, and that the shame of thy nakedness do not appear; and anoint thine eyes with eyesalve, that thou mayest see, [19] As many as I love, I rebuke and chasten: be zealous therefore, and repent."* – **Revelation 3:18-19**
    b.　Their character
        1.　Poverty **(vs. 17)**
- Wretched
- Miserable
- Poor
- Blind
- Naked

    c.　Their remedy **(vs. 18)**
        1.　Gold
- God's righteousness

        2.　White raiment
- Righteousness of the saints makes free from the shame of nakedness

        3.　Eyesalve **(vs. 18)**
- Spiritual discernment

        4.　Repentance **(vs. 19)**

IX.　LAST CALL – vs. 20
    a.　*"Behold, I stand at the door and knock: if any man hear my voice, and open the door, I will come in to him, and will sup with him, and he with me."* – **Revelation 3:20**
    b.　**"Behold"** is the word of John the Baptist at the beginning of the New Testament in **John 1:36 "Behold the Lamb of God"**. Christ was great in the estimation of heaven, and was manifested before the eyes of mankind for close scrutiny.
    c.　The Lord would attract to Himself His disciples, and draw them away from the business and social life that occupied them. This appeal is to every believer today who is caught up in the fast pace of modern living that leaves little or no time for the work of God.

EPISODES OF THE END, THE REVELATION OF JESUS CHRIST

    d.   **"...the door..." (vs. 20)**
        1.   The door would speak of the responsibility to hear and open.
    e.   **"...and knock..." (vs. 20)**
        1.   He knocks, but speaks of hearing His voice rather than His knock. This signifies that all restoration is by the Word of God.
        2.   It is the Word of God that makes wise unto salvation and all recovery is likewise by the Word of God.
    f.   The promise
        1.   **"...I will come in to him, and will sup with him,..." (vs. 20)**
            • This speaks of fellowship as with a meal around a table.
        2.   **"...and he with me." (vs. 20)**
            • This speaks of the Lord's joy and delight in the communion with His saints.

X.   <u>**OVERCOMERS REWARD**</u> **– vs. 21**
    a.   *"To him that overcometh will I grant to sit with Me in my Throne, even as I also overcame, and am set down with My Father in His throne."* **– Revelation 3:21**
    b.   Christ assures the overcomers of the glorious reward.
        1.   As He now shares His Father's throne, they will be identified with his throne, and thus, share in His glorious millennial reign.
            • *"**Blessed and holy is he hat hath part in the first resurrection: on such the second death hath no power, but they shall be priests of God and of Christ, and shall reign with Him a thousand years.**"* **– Revelation 20:6**

XI. **FINAL APPEAL – vs. 22**
    a.   *"He that hath an ear, let him hear what the Spirit saith unto the churches."* **– Revelation 3:22**
    b.   In the seventh letter, for the seventh time, Christ cries *"He that hath an ear, let him hear what the Spirit saith unto the churches"*.
    c.   What yearning it evidences on the part of God to enrich the individual with His best in time and eternity.

Up to this point, we have been occupied with the history of the Church on the earth in chapters 2 and 3. The Church age has run it's course and has been raptured to heaven.

> Remember God's three-point outline of Revelation is as follows:

I.   Things which thou hast seen in Chapter 1
II.   Things which are in Chapters 2 and 3.
III.   Things which shall be hereafter in Chapters 4 through 22.

Before we begin the study on "the things which shall be hereafter", let us look at Daniel, Chapter nine (9) and the seventy (70) weeks. The seventy (70) weeks are weeks of years, which is four-hundred ninety (490) years. Sixty-nine (69) weeks have already been fulfilled, which is four-hundred eighty three (483) years when Christ presented Himself to Israel as their Messiah Prince. This leaves the last week or one week of Daniel to be fulfilled which is in the future and will be the Great Tribulation. There is a gap of time between the sixty-ninth (69) and seventieth (70) week of Daniel, which is the Church age. So, we are in the "gap" of the sixty-ninth (69) and seventieth (70) week of Daniel today. There is more discussion of this on in this chapter.

Daniel Chapter nine (9) may be divided into three (3) distinct parts.

I. **DANIEL'S STUDY OF THE PROPHECY OF JEREMIAH – vs. 1-2**
   a. *" [1] In the first year of Darius the son of Ahasuerus, of the seed of the Medes, which was made king over the realm of the Chaldeans; [2] In the first year of his reign I Daniel understood by books the number of the years, whereof the word of the LORD came to Jeremiah the prophet, that he would accomplish seventy years in the desloations of Jerusalem." – Daniel 9:1-2*
   b. Daniel understood from the book of Jeremiah that the Babylonian captivity of the Jews was coming to a close.
      1. *" [11] And this whole land shall be a desolation, and an astonishment; and these nations shall serve the king of Babylon seventy years. [12] And it shall come to pass, when seventy years are accomplished, that I will punish the king of Babylon, and that nation, saith the LORD, for their iniquity, and the land of the Chaldeans, and will make it perpetual desolations." – Jeremiah 25:11-12*
      2. *"For thus saith the LORD, That after seventy years be accomplished at Babylon I will visit you, and perform my good word toward you, in causing you to return to this place." – Jeremiah 29:10*

II. **DANIEL'S PRAYER FOR THE FULFILLMENT OF THE PROPHECY – vs. 3-19**
   a. Read **Daniel 9:3-19**
   b. Daniel's confession of the sins of Israel and his own sin.

III. **GOD'S ANSWER TO DANIEL'S PRAYER – vs. 20-25**
   a. Read **Daniel 9:20-25**
   b. The answer was the seventy weeks revealed

1. Among the Hebrews there were three (3) classifications of weeks.
   - Week of days – from one Sabbath to another
     ❖ **Genesis 2:2**
   - Weeks of years – from one Sabbatical year to another Sabbatical year
     ❖ **Genesis 29:27**
     ❖ **Numbers 14:34**
   - Weeks of seven times seven years, or forty-nine (49) years
     ❖ **Leviticus 25:8-13**

As stated above, Chapter 9 in Daniel is divided into three (3) distinct parts. Following are those parts.

I. <u>THE SEVENTY WEEKS OF YEARS ARE FOUR-HUNDRED NINETY (490) YEARS</u> – vs. 24

a. *"Seventy weeks are determined upon thy people and upon thy holy city, to finish the transgression, and to make an end of sins, and to make reconciliation for iniquity, and to bring in everlasting righteousness, and to seal up the vision and prophecy, and to anoint the most Holy."* – **Daniel 9:24**

b. Here the Hebrew word "seventy" is translated "weeks" as demanded by the context. But, the word means "seventy sevens". So we understand that the prophecy in this verse relates to seventy (70) sevens (7) or four-hundred ninety (490) years. 70 weeks times 7 years equals 490 years.

c. That years, not days or months, are meant is evident from the fact that Daniel was thinking in terms of years as the angel, Gabriel, came to speak to him. **(Daniel 9:2)**

d. The purpose of the seventy weeks
   1. *"Seventy weeks are determined upon thy people and upon thy holy city, to finish the transgression, and to make an end of sins,*

and to make reconciliation for iniquity, and to bring in everlasting righteousness, and to seal up the vision and prophecy, and to anoint the most Holy." – **Daniel 9:24**

2. The angel, Gabriel, first summarized what was to transpire in the seventy (70) weeks of years by listing six (6) important purposes of God's relating to the people, Israel, and to the Holy City, Jerusalem.
   - To Finish the Transgression
     - The word transgression means "rebel". It refers to the Jews specific sin of rebellion against the rule of God. Deep rebellion brought deep affliction.
   - To Make and End of Sins
     - That is, to put an end to daily sins of God's people
   - To Make Reconciliation for Iniquity
     - That is, to provide atonement for sin
   - To Bring in Everlasting Righteousness
     - That is, to bring in a kingdom in which everlasting righteousness will prevail. This is a millennial characteristic, deriving from the blood of Christ. After Christ's crucifixion, He had nothing – **Daniel 9:26**. But, in that future day, Israel will no longer be seeking after righteousness according to the law – **Romans 9:31; 10:3**, but will have *"life from death"* – **Romans 11:15**.
   - To Seal Up the Vision and Prophecy
     - That is, to bring to completion by fulfillment all prophecies of Scripture. The word translated "to seal up" is the same word which was translated "to make an end" in the phrase "to make an end of sins" earlier in this verse. It would appear that there is an intended

relationship between the two phrases. The relationship is as follows:
- ♦ When Israel will make an end of it's daily sins at the end of the 490 years, then all revelation that came through vision and prophecy concerning God's chastening of Israel can be sealed up.
- To Anoint the Most Holy
  - ❖ That is, to anoint the religious service, the most Holy place, of as yet future, the Millennial Temple. This will not be a Temple of types and shadows as in the Old Testament, but one for service with the Lord present.
    - ♦ *" [4] And the glory of the LORD came into the house by the way of the gate whose prospect is toward the east. [5] So the spirit took me up, and brought me into the inner court; and, behold, the glory of the LORD filled the house."* – Ezekiel 43:4-5

II. THE BEGINNING OF THE SEVENTY (70) WEEKS – vs. 25 and Nehemiah 2:1-8

a. *"Know therefore and understand, that from the going forth of the commandment to restore and to build Jerusalem unto the Messiah the Prince shall be seven weeks, and threescore and two weeks: the street shall be built again, and the wall, even in troublous times."* – Daniel 9:25

b. We have seventy (70) weeks in verse 24. Gabriel explains that the (70) seventy weeks are divided into three (3) sections in verses 24 and 25.

   1. <u>Seven (7) Weeks of Years (49 Years)</u>

- During this period, 49 years (or the 7 weeks), the city of Jerusalem was rebuilt. The street and the wall was rebuilt again, even in troublous times. Under the leadership of Nehemiah, the walls of the city were repaired in fifty-two (52) days **(Nehemiah 6:15)**. It apparently took much longer to clear out all of the debris and restore all of the damage inflicted by Nebuchadnezzar. The seventy (70) weeks began with **Nehemiah 2:1-8**.

2. Sixty-two (62) Weeks (434 Years)
   - The second period sweeps on to Christ, the "Messiah the Prince". After the 49 years (or the 7 weeks) period, there was another period of 434 years (or the 62 weeks) before the Messiah came as the Prince of Israel. The first cycle of the 49 years, while mentioned separately from the 434 years, is yet joined to it, therefore, making the two cycles combined totaling 483 years. This brings us to the first coming of Christ. Not however to His birth, but apparently to the day He presented Himself to the nation of Israel as their Messiah Prince. In an official manner He did this only once at the time of the triumphal entry into Jerusalem **(Matthew 21:1-11)**. This event fulfilled 69 weeks (or 483 years) of Daniel's 70 weeks (or 490 years).
   ❖ What happens after the 69th week?
      ♦ This question is answered in verse 26.
         I. ***"And after threescore and two weeks shall Messiah be cut off, but not for Himself: and the people of the Prince that shall come shall destroy the city and the sanctuary; and the end thereof shall be with a flood, and unto the end of the war desolations are determined." Daniel 9:26***

REVELATION—CHAPTER 3

- ♦ It should be noted that there is a gap now introduced between the 69th and 70th week because of several very significant events predicted to come to pass after 62 weeks following the first 7 weeks, making a total of 69 weeks or 483 years.

I. <u>Messiah will be cut off – Christ crucified</u>
   "He came unto His own, and His own received Him not." – John 1:11

II. <u>The city and sanctuary will be destroyed</u>
   a. *"...and the end thereof shall be with a flood,..."* – **(Daniel 9:26)**. The flood refers back to the destruction of Jerusalem (70 AD).
   b. History records that Titus, the Roman General, led four (4) Roman legions to besiege and destroy Jerusalem in 70 AD.
   c. Verse 26 also states that both the city and sanctuary would be destroyed by "the people of the prince who is to come". Interestingly enough, "the people" or the Romans have already come, yet "the prince" or the anti-Christ is still yet to come. The prince cannot refer to the Messiah Prince in verse 25 since the date of His coming was already carefully determined. Rather, this refers to a future prince, or the anti-Christ, who was referred to in **Daniel Chapter 7:8, 19, and 26**.

III. <u>War and Desolation will be the continuing experience of the people of Israel</u> – **vs. 26**
   a. ** GAP PERIOD OF TIME HERE **
   b. The gap period began when Christ made His triumphal entry into Jerusalem **(Matthew 21:1-11)**.

believe the latter part of verse 26 ***"...and unto the end of the war desolations are determined."*** is in the gap period. This interval is a period of time unknown and it has lasted approximately 2000 years.

    c. This "gap" period of time is the Church age. There will be wars and desolation for the duration of the Church age. This will be, and is currently, perilous times **(II Timothy 3:1-8)**. God is now calling a people out of the world to Himself, which make up the body of Christ, or the Church. We do not know how much longer this period will last. The Church age will end with the return of Christ to receive unto Himself His own **(I Thessalonians 4:16-17)**.

3. Seventieth (70th) Week (7 years)

    a. Thus, the 70th week, or the last 7 years of the 490 years involved in the prophecy, did not follow immediately after the end of the first 69 weeks, or 483 years. This indicates that the 7 years of tribulation period has not yet begun.

    b. There is nothing unusual about this "gap" period of time found here in **Daniel 9:26-27**. Another example of such a "gap" is found in **Luke 4:18-19** where Jesus reads from **Isaiah 61:2**. He stops reading in the middle of **Isaiah 61:2**.

    1. ***"To proclaim the acceptable year of the LORD..."*** **- Isaiah 61:2(a).**

• This part of this verse was fulfilled in the day of Jesus. This is Christ's first advent.

• Where the comma is indicates the "gap" of time here in **Isaiah 61:2**.

2. *"...and the day of vengeance of our God; to comfort all that mourn;"* – **Isaiah 61:2(b).**
- This latter part of this verse is yet future. This will be Christ's second advent.
- **I Thessalonians 1:7-10**

c. The Church age lies between the 69th and 70th week of Daniel. The next thing on God's program is the rapture of the Church. The Church age ends with Revelation, Chapter 3, the Laodicea Church.

d. The Rapture of the Church

1. *"After this I looked, and, behold, a door was opened in heaven: and the first voice which I heard was as it were of a trumpet talking with me; which said, Come up hither, and I will shew thee things which must be hereafter."* – **Revelation 4:1**

2. *"After this"* means after the Church age is over. At this point, John sees a door open in heaven and hears a voice as it were a trumpet talking with him saying *"Come up hither"* (this is the rapture), *and I will shew thee things which must be hereafter."* If John, in the vision, is to see the happenings on earth, he must see them from heaven. He cannot view them being in the midst. **John's position in heaven**, is surely typical of the position the Church will have when the tribulation judgements begin to fall on the earth. This is quite in line with the truth that the Church will NOT go through the tribulation.

III. THE 70TH WEEK – vs. 27

a. *"And he shall confirm the covenant with many for one week: and in the midst of the week he shall cause the sacrifice and the oblation to cease, and for the overspreading of abominations he shall make it desolate, even until the consummation, and that determined shall be poured upon the desolate."* – Daniel 9:27

b. The Seven Year Covenant
1. The 70th week (7 years) begins after the Church has been caught up to Heaven **(I Thessalonians 4:17)**.
2. The anti-Christ will make a covenant with many (the Jews) the first 3 ½ years of the tribulation to protect them from their enemies.

c. The Covenant Broken
1. In the midst of the 7 years, the anti-Christ will break the covenant with the Jews, causing the sacrifice (in the restored temple – vs. 27) to cease and desecrate the temple and will claim to be God and demand to be worshipped as God **(II Thessalonians 2:4)**.
2. The abomination in verse 27 is the same that Jesus spoke of in **Matthew 24:15**. "The abominations" are detested "things" connected with idolatry, here with the horrors of the anti-Christ, *"Who opposeth and exalteth himself above all that is called God, or that is worshipped; so that he as God sitteth in the temple of God shewing himself that he is God"* **(II Thessalonians 2:4)**. The anti-Christ will turn on the Jews, and they will flee into the mountains for refuge **(Matthew 24:16)**.
3. The final period of 1 week (or 7 years) is dominated by the appearance of the anti-Christ who becomes the Jews protector and then their persecutor until he is stopped by Christ on His return to earth **(Revelation 19:20)**.
4. The 7 year tribulation period runs from **Revelation chapter 6 through chapter 19**.

Revelation – Chapter 4

The Things Which Shall Be Hereafter

Up to this point, we have been occupied with the history of the Church on earth. In Chapters 2 and 3, the Church age has run its course. In Revelation 1:19, we have a three fold division of Revelation.

- "Write the things which thou hast seen…"
    - ❖ John does this in Chapter 1.
- "…And things which are…".
    - ❖ John writes these in Chapters 2 and 3.
- "…And the things which shall be hereafter…"
    - ❖ This begins with Chapter 4 through Chapter 22.

I. **THE RAPTURE** – vs. 1-2

    a.   **"[1] After this I looked, and, behold, a door was opened in Heaven: and the first voice which I heard was as it were of a trumpet talking with me; which said Come up hither, and I will shew thee things which must be hereafter. [2] And immediately I was in the Spirit: and, behold, a throne was set in Heaven, and One sat on the throne."** – Revelation 4:1-2

    b.   Notice four things that John mentions here:
        1.   The open door of Heaven
        2.   The Voice
        3.   The Trumpet
        4.   The Invitation "come up"

    c.   These are the same things mentioned by Paul when he speaks of the Lord coming for His Church in **I Thessalonians 4:16-17 and II Corinthians 15:52**.

    d.   The calling of John up into Heaven was a type of the "calling" (or rapture) of the Church into Heaven.

    e.   The Voice John heard is described as being like a trumpet. This fits the description of the rapture mentioned in **I Thessalonians 4:16** where Paul

- f. ***"And immediately I was in the Spirit:..."* (vs. 2)**
    1. The word "immediately" means "at once" or "without delay".
    2. This corresponds exactly with the teachings concerning the Rapture which takes place at once, *"in a moment, in the twinkling of an eye"* – I Corinthians 15:52.
- g. The Rapture Will Be Secret
    1. As to the time of Christ's coming for His Church, it will be sudden and unannounced. No advance warning will be given. This is made clear in **Luke 12:36-40**.
    2. For those who refused Christ before the rapture, they will perish under the rule of the anti-Christ. There will be no second chance for salvation after the rapture has taken place for anyone who understood and was enlightened by the Holy Spirit and the Word of God before the return of Christ. Therefore, it is desperately urgent for all people who have had an opportunity to receive Christ to do so today and believe on Him for salvation before He returns.
        - *"...behold, now is the day of salvation."* – II Corinthians 6:2
        - *"For whosoever shall call upon the Name of the Lord shall be saved."* – **Romans 10:13**
    3. I am aware of the scripture fact that a great multitude will be saved during the tribulation period. A great multitude made up of all tribes, tongues, kindred, and people of the earth (Revelation 7:9-14), but those who will be saved are those who have never heard the Gospel of truth. There are millions on earth today who have never heard the Gospel of salvation.
- h. The Rapture Will Be Sudden
    1. *"In a moment, in the twinkling of an eye..."* – **I Corinthians 15:52**

REVELATION—CHAPTER 4

        2.   The blink of an eye takes about 1/10 of a second. The nerve impulse causes the blink reflex to travel at approximately 30 miles per hour. In that short of a time, all Christians will leave the earth to be with Christ.

  i. <u>The Rapture Will Be Selective</u>
        1.   **"...and the dead in Christ shall rise first:" – I Thessalonians 4:16**
        2.   The selective ones are all those, whether dead or alive, who have received Christ.

  j. <u>The Rapture Will Be Sure</u>
        1.   **"For this we say unto you by the Word of the Lord,..." – I Thessalonians 4:15**
        2.   The Word of God is:
- Sure
  - **Psalm 111:7**
  - **Matthew 5:18**
- Eternal
  - **Matthew 24:35**
  - **Psalm 119:89**
- Food for the Soul
  - **Job 23:12**
  - **Psalm 119:103**
  - **Jeremiah 15:16**
- Comfort for the Saints
  - **I Thessalonians 4:18**
  - **Romans 15:4**

II. <u>THE REDEEMER</u> – vs. 2
  a. **"...and One sat on the throne." – Revelation 4:2**
  b. This is God Himself.
  c. Job calls Him "My Redeemer"
      1.   **"For I know that my Redeemer liveth..." – Job 19:25**

III. THE RAINBOW – vs. 3
   a. *"And He that sat was to look upon like a jasper and a sardine stone: and there was a rainbow round about the throne, in sight like unto an emerald."* **– Revelation 4:3**
   b. The rainbow was first mentioned in **Genesis 9:13**. God pledged to Noah that He would never destroy the earth again by water.
   c. God has another pledge with His Son, and He is about to fulfill it. He promised that one day the earth would be Christ's footstool.
      1. **Psalm 110:1**
      2. **Acts 2:34-35**
   d. The rainbow symbolized God's mercy, grace, and covenant promised in the midst of Divine Judgement.
      1. **Genesis 9:13**
   e. For the saved, the storm is over since Christ bore the judgement for our sins at Calvary. Here judgement is about to begin preparing the earth for Christ's return.

IV. THE REPRESENTATIVES – vs. 4
   a. *"And round about the throne were four and twenty seats: and upon the seats I saw four and twenty elders sitting, clothed in white raiment; and they had on their heads crowns of gold."* **– Revelation 4:4**
   b. Who are these 24 elders?
      1. They are the redeemed ones
         - **Revelation 5:8-9**
      2. In **I Chronicles 24:1-19**, there were 24 elders appointed by King David to represent the entire priesthood. The elders represent all the redeemed who have died in the Lord of all the ages.
      3. It is an all inclusive number showing that all of God's people, without exception, will be there.
         - They are clothed in white.
            ❖ White means the perfect righteousness of Christ.
         - On their heads crowns of gold

REVELATION—CHAPTER 4

- ❖ Royal dignity
- ❖ Reward for service

V. **THE RUMBLING** – vs. 5
    a. *"And out of the throne proceeded lightnings and thunderings and voices: and there were seven lamps of fire burning before the throne, which are the seven Spirits of God."* – **Revelation 4:5**
    b. The storm is about to break. Judgement is coming.
    c. Seven lamps of fire burning shows the Holy Spirit taking on a judicial character.
    d. This is not a throne of mercy or grace. It is a throne of judgement.

VI. **THE RENDERERS** – vs. 6-11
    a. *"[6] And before the throne there was a sea of glass like unto crystal: and in the midst of the throne, and round about the throne, were four beasts full of eyes before and behind. [7] And the first beast was like a lion, and the second beast like a calf, and the third beast had a face as a man, and the fourth beast was like a flying eagle. [8] And the four beasts had each of them six wings about him; and they were full of eyes within: and they rest not day and night, saying Holy, holy, holy, Lord God Almighty, which was, and is, and is to come. [9] And when those beasts give glory and honor and thanks to him that sat on the throne, who liveth for ever and ever, [10] The four and twenty elders fall down before him that sat on the throne, and worship him that liveth for ever and ever, and cast their crowns before the throne, saying, [11] Thou art worthy, O Lord, to receive glory and honor and power: for Thou hast created all things, and for Thy pleasure they are and were created."* – **Revelation 4:6-11**
    b. The laver in the tabernacle **(Exodus 30:18-21)**, and the sea in Solomon's temple **(I Kings 7:23-27)** was where the priests washed themselves before they served in the tabernacle.

- c. Water is a type of God's Word. But in Heaven, the sea is solid. Heaven is a fixed state of holiness, purity, and perfection. Now, in Heaven, the people do not need to wash. They are clean and can worship God continually. While on earth, God's people are cleansed by the Word **(John 15:3)**.
- d. The Four Beasts
  1. Scholars are divided on who and what the living creatures represent.
  2. The word beast here means, "living creatures".
  3. Some see them as angels. Others believe they may represent the attributes of God:
     - Majesty
     - Strength
     - Intelligence
     - Divine Vigilance
  4. Still others see them as reflecting the four aspects of Christ's ministry in the Gospels.
  5. The most reasonable view is that John saw some type of angelic beings. Ezekiel saw such living creatures **(Ezekiel 1:5-14)**. He called them Cherubims **(Ezekiel 10:14-22)**. They are similar to the Seraphims mentioned in **Isaiah 6:2-3**.
  6. I believe these living creatures are some order of angelic beings whose sole function is to render glory, honor, thanks, praise, and service to God. This is what every believer should do.

VII. **THE RECEIVER – vs. 11**
- a. *"Thou art worthy, O Lord, to receive glory and honor and power: for Thou hast created all things, and for Thy pleasure they are and were created." –* **Revelation 4:11**
- b. Christ is the receiver of all praise, glory, and honor.
- c. Not only are we to praise God for saving us, but also for creating us.
- d. The first subject revealed in the Bible is that of creation.
  1. **Genesis 1:1**
- e. It is the first in which faith is demanded.

1. **Hebrews 11:3**
2. **John 1:3**
3. **Colossians 1:16**

f. There are no songs of evolution in Heaven, only songs of creation.

Revelation – Chapter 5

In Chapter Five (5), John continues to describe the scene, which met his eyes when he was caught up to Glory. Chapters 4 and 5 are one scene.

The Seven Sealed Book

I. **THE SEALED BOOK – vs. 1-2**
   a. *"[1] And I saw in the right hand of Him that sat on the throne a book written within and on the backside, sealed with seven seals. [2] And I saw a strong angel proclaiming with a loud voice, Who is worthy to open the book, and to loose the seals thereof?" – Revelation 5:1-2*
   b. The seal is the mark of ownership and has to do with title deeds.
      1. **Jeremiah 32:7-12**
   c. The seven-sealed Book contains the Judgements of the seven-year tribulation, the sum total of perfection and Divine completeness.
   d. The Book contains the title deed to the earth.
      1. **"The earth is the Lord's, and the fulness thereof; the world, and they that dwell therein." – Psalm 24:1**
      2. Adam sold out the human race. Man and the earth were lost to sin. Jesus bought it back. He is our kinsman Redeemer.
      3. Redemption is not confined alone to Christ's first coming to earth, but also to His Second Coming.
- **"And when these things begin to come to pass, then look up, and lift up your heads; for your redemption draweth nigh." – Luke 21:28**
- In the Church age, believers are sealed with the Holy Spirit.

> ❖ *"[13] In whom ye also trusted, after that ye heard the Word of truth, the Gospel of your salvation: in whom also after that ye believed, ye were sealed with that Holy Spirit of promise, [14] Which is the earnest of our inheritance until the redemption of the purchased possession, unto the praise of His glory."* – **Ephesians 1:13-14**

- The possession has been purchased, but not fully redeemed. All creation groans and is waiting to be redeemed.
  > ❖ *"For we know that the whole creation groaneth and travaileth in pain together until now."* – **Romans 8:22**
- The Saints are awaiting the redemption of the body.
  > ❖ *"And not only they, but ourselves also, which have the first-fruits of the Spirit, even we ourselves groan within ourselves, waiting for the adoption, to wit, the redemption of our body."* – **Romans 8:23**

There are three (3) laws of Redemption:

1. Concerning a Wife
- **Deuteronomy 25:5-10**
- If her husband died leaving no children, the husband's brother was to take his widow so that his name would not die. But he must first be able to support her. If he were not financially able to care for the widow, he had no right to take her.
- Jesus, with His own blood bought the bride **(Acts 20:28)**. Jesus was able and He was the only one who could redeem man. The woman is a type of the Church.

2. Concerning a Slave
- **Deuteronomy 15:12**
- If a man lost all his possessions and could not pay his debts, his creditors could take him as a slave. (Adam lost it all when he sinned, and therefore, we became slaves to sin.) When the slave had served six (6) years, he could go free **(Deuteronomy 15:12)**.
- Man has been a slave to sin and Satan since Adam's fall. But, Jesus has paid the ransom note for us with His own precious blood **(Acts 20:28, I Peter 1:18-19)**.
  - ❖ *"If the Son, therefore, shall make you free, ye shall be free indeed." – John 8:36*

3. Concerning the Land
- **Leviticus 25:23-25**
- In verse 23, God says, "the land is mine".
- *"If thy brother be waxen poor, and hath sold away some of his possession, and if any of his kin come to redeem it, then shall he redeem that which his brother sold." – (vs. 25)*
- If a poor brother lost his property because of poverty, it could be redeemed back by either two (2) ways:
  a. The owner could pay the redemption price. But how could he ever pay the debt? He was a slave because of the debt, and being a slave, he could never earn enough money to pay the debt.
  b. A near kinsman could redeem the land and pay the debt while the original owner was in slavery.
- The first Adam sold out to Satan; the second Adam, (Christ), bought back with His own blood, what the first Adam lost. When God cursed Adam, He cursed all creation – man, the animal kingdom, and the vegetable kingdom – all creation. When Adam fell, all fell. *"[17] ...cursed is the ground for thy sake; in sorrow shalt thou eat of it all the days of thy life; [18] Thorns also and thistles shall it bring forth to thee; and thou shalt eat the herb of the field;" – Genesis 3:17(b)-18*
- In Leviticus chapter 25, two (2) of these redemptions have been fulfilled.

REVELATION—CHAPTER 5

    a. The wife has been redeemed – the New Testament Church – Jesus purchased with His own blood **(Acts 20:28)**.
    b. The slave has been redeemed **(Ephesians 1:7)**. He will save us from the slavery of sinful bodies in the rapture **(I Thessalonians 4:13-18 and I Corinthians 15:51-53)**.

The only redemption not yet accomplished in the law of redemption in Israel is the Land. Jesus will redeem the land when He comes with His Saints at the end of the seven-year tribulation **(Revelation 19:11-21)**.

II. THE SEEKING AND SORROW – vs. 3-4

    a. *"[3] And no man in heaven, nor in earth, neither under the earth, was able to open the book, neither to look thereon. [4] And I wept much, because no man was found worthy to open and to read the book, neither to look thereon."* – **Revelation 5:3-4**
    b. Three kingdoms were searched
        1. Heaven – no angel was worthy
        2. Earth – no man was worthy
        3. Under the earth – none was worthy
- Under the earth means Hell (Hades), the place of dead people and also demons or wicked spirits. None of these could open the scroll.
- John knew everything depended upon finding someone worthy to be kinsman redeemer to open the seven seals. John knew the meaning of the sealed book. He knew it was the complete and final redemption of man, of Israel, and of the earth.

Christ in His Kingly Character Opens the Book

EPISODES OF THE END, THE REVELATION OF JESUS CHRIST

III.   **THE SUCCESS** – vs. 5-7

    a.   *"[5] And one of the elders saith unto me, Weep not: behold, the Lion of the tribe of Juda, the Root of David, hath prevailed to open the book and to loose the seven seals thereof. [6] And I beheld, and lo, in the midst of the throne and of the four beasts, and in the midst of the elder, stood a Lamb as it had been slain, having seven horns and seven eyes, which are the seven Spirits of God sent forth into all the earth. [7] And he came and took the book out of the right hand of him that sat upon the throne."* – Revelation 5:5-7

    b.   John's weeping was for a short duration. One was found who was able to open the scroll.

        1.   The Lion of the tribe of Juda
- Jesus, in His Lion like character, crushes all opposing forces.

        2.   The Root of David
- As the Root of David, He is the Great Kinsman Redeemer who alone is worthy to open the scroll.

        3.   The Slain Lamb
- As the slain Lamb, He has the right to claim what He (the Kinsman Redeemer) has purchased.
    - ❖ In His Lion like character, it refers to His
        a. Second Coming
        b. Majesty
        c. Sovereignty
        d. Right to Judge
        e. Government of God
    - ❖ In His Lamb like character, it refers to His
        a. First Coming
        b. Meekness
        c. Savior
        d. As the Lamb, He is Judged (slain)
        e. Speaks of the Grace of God

REVELATION—CHAPTER 5

> The Living Creatures Worship Because of Redemption

IV. **THE SAINTS PRAYERS** – vs. 8
    a. *"And when He had taken the book, the four beasts and four and twenty elders fell down before the Lamb, having every one of them harps, and golden vials full of odours, which are the prayers of the saints."* – **Revelation 5:8**
    b. No real prayer is ever lost or forgotten.

V. **THE SONG** – vs. 9-10
    a. *"[9] And they sung a new song, saying, Thou art worthy to take the book, and to open the seals thereof: for thou wast slain, and hast redeemed us to God by thy blood out of every kindred, and tongue, and people, and nation; [10] And hast made us unto our God kings and priests: and we shall reign on the earth."* – **Revelation 5:9-10**
    b. The song was new because of its theme; redemption not typically, but actually accomplished. It was new because it was sung in Heaven on the eve of the full burst of the millennial joy. We shall reign on the earth.

> The Angel Exalts the Lamb

VI. **THE SHOUTING** – vs. 11-12
    a. *"[11] And I beheld, and I heard the voice of many angels round about the throne and the beasts and the elders: and the number of them was ten thousand times ten thousand, and thousands of thousands; [12] Saying with a loud voice, Worthy is the Lamb that was slain to receive power, and riches, and wisdom, and strength, and honour, and glory, and blessing."* – **Revelation 5:11-12**
    b. *"...Saying with a loud voice..."* **(vs. 12)** – In Heaven, angels and the entire redeemed yield to God's authority. Do we now?

c. A seven (7) fold ascription to the Lamb
     1. Power – omnipotence – **vs. 12**
     2. Riches – possessions – **vs. 12 and John 17:5**
     3. Wisdom – omniscience – **vs. 12**
     4. Strength – ability – **vs. 12 and Hebrews 7:25**
     5. Honor – reputation – **vs. 12 and Hebrews 1:4**
     6. Glory – praise – **vs. 12 and Philippians 2:9-11**
     7. Blessing – worship – **vs. 12**

Universal Adoration of the Lamb

VII. <u>THE SOUND</u> – vs. 13-14
  a. *"[13] And every creature which is in heaven, and on the earth, and under the earth, and such as are in the sea, and all that are in them, heard I saying, Blessing, and honor, and glory, and power, be unto Him that sitteth upon the throne, and unto the Lamb for ever and ever. [14] And the four beasts said, Amen. And the four and twenty elders fell down and worshipped Him that liveth for ever and ever."* – **Revelation 5:13-14**
  b. The message of praise rolls on gathering force and volume. Creatures in heaven, on the earth, under the earth, and such as are in the sea.
     1. Sinners (under the earth) and Saints will unite in the glad declaration.
     2. Every created intelligence will never cease praising Him forever and ever.
        - Celestial
        - Terrestrial
        - Infernal – **Phillippians 2:10-11**
     3. People on the earth in the tribulation will say, "The Saints were right."
     4. In Hell forever and ever **(vs. 13)**, people in hell will continuously admit, "He is Worthy".

Revelation – Chapter 6

Chapters six through eleven (6-11) present the Judgements of the seven (7) seals and the seven (7) trumpets. Bear in mind the following facts:

- These Judgements will fall upon the unbelieving earth – dweller after the Church is gone.
- The author outlines the Judgements of the Seals. He describes six (6) of the Seal Judgements in Revelation chapter six (6). Then he inserts a connector pause, a parenthetical section (Revelation 8:1). Then the climax is reached in chapter eight (8) with the seventh (7th) seal, which introduces, as by a chain reaction, the next series of the seven (7) trumpet Judgements.

The First Seal

I. **THE SEALS** – vs. 1-2
- a. *"[1] And I saw when the Lamb opened one of the seals, and I heard, as it were the noise of thunder, one of the four beasts saying, Come and see. [2] And I saw, and behold a white horse: and he that sat on him had a bow; and a crown was given unto him: and he went forth conquering, and to conquer."* – Revelation 6:1-2
- b. The First (1st) Seal (vs. 1-2)
   1. *"...as it were a noise of thunder..."* (vs. 1)
   2. Judgement is about to break forth. The storm is coming.

II. **THE SATANIC IMITATOR** – vs. 2
- a. This is the anti-Christ imitating Christ by way of contrast with the rider (Christ) of **Revelation 19:11**.
- b. This is man's last effort to bring order and peace to the world while Christ is still rejected.
- c. What Napoleon, Kaiser Bill, Hitler, Joseph Stalin, and many others failed to do by force, the anti-Christ will do by:

1. Flattery
   - **Daniel 11:21-35**
   - Antiochus Epiphanes – a type of the anti-Christ
2. Deception
   - **II Thessalonians 2:9-12**
   - **John 5:43**
3. Delusion
   - **Daniel 11:36-45**
   - **II Thessalonians 2:3-12**
4. Had a Bow
   - Cold War
5. Crown given to him
   - The word here for crown is "stephanos", the victors' crown as given in the Olympic Games. It is not the "diadem" worn by Christ in **Revelation 19:12**. The diadem is the kingly crown. Jesus is our King **(Revelation 19:16)**.

d. The anti-Christ is a brilliant, strategically, irresistible conqueror.
   1. *"...all the world wondered after the beast..."* – **Revelation 13:3-8**

The Second Seal

II. <u>**THE SORROWS**</u> – vs. 3-4
   a. *"[3] And when He had opened the second seal, I heard the second beast say, Come and see. [4] And there went out another horse that was red: and power was given to him that sat thereon to take peace from the earth, and that they should kill one another: and there was given unto him a great sword."* – Revelation 6:3-4
   b. <u>The Second (2nd) Seal</u> **(vs. 3)**
      1. Wars

- Universal war breaks upon the world. The horse is the symbol for swift aggressive warfare.
- Red is the color of blood and speaks of war, bloodshed, suffering, sorrow, and conflict.

2. Race Wars
3. Class Wars
4. Religious Wars
- *"And I will call for a sword against him throughout all my mountains, saith the Lord God: every man's sword shall be against his brother." – Ezekiel 38:21*

The Third Seal

III. THE SCARCITY OF FOOD – vs. 5-6

a. *"[5] And when He had opened the third seal, I heard the third beast say, Come and see. And I beheld, and lo a black horse; and he that sat on him had a pair of balances in his hand. [6] And I heard a voice in the midst of the four beasts say, A measure of wheat for a penny, and three measures of barley for a penny; and see thou hurt not the oil and the wine." – Revelation 6:5-6*

b. The Third (3rd) Seal **(vs. 5)**

   1. Famine always follows war. Today, thousands of people are starving to death, but it cannot be compared with what is to come.
      - *"They that be slain with the sword are better than they that be slain with hunger: for these pine away, stricken through for want of the fruits of the field." – Lamentations 4:9*
   2. In the Bible, famine is symbolized by the color black.
      - *"Our skin was black like an oven because of the terrible famine." – Lamentations 5:10*

3. A measure of wheat equals about one quart. There are thirty-two (32) quarts in a bushel. In Bible times, a penny (or a Roman denarius) was the amount for a day's wage for a soldier or a laboring man.
   - **Matthew 20:2-9**
4. In 1990, the average day's wage was about $60.00 per day. Let's assume that in the tribulation time, a day's wage will be $60.00 per day. A bushel of wheat would cost $1,920.00 per bushel. A bushel of barley would cost $640.00 per bushel.
5. It will be a time of famine and of death.
6. The rich or wealthy will be spared.
   - *"...and see thou hurt not the oil and the wine."* **(vs. 6)**
   - Oil and wine were regarded as luxuries.
     - ❖ **Proverbs 21:17**
     - ❖ **Jeremiah 31:12**
     - ❖ **Psalm 104:15**

The Fourth Seal

IV. THE STROKE OF DEATH – vs. 7-8

a. *"[7] And when He had opened the fourth seal, I heard the voice of the fourth beast say, Come and see. [8] And I looked, and behold a pale horse: and his name that sat on him was Death, and Hell followed with him. And power was given unto them over the fourth part of the earth, to kill with sword, and with hunger, and with death, and with the beasts of the earth."* – **Revelation 6:7-8**

b. The Fourth (4th) Seal **(vs. 7)**
   1. The word "death" is used twice in verse 8. The second word "death" means pestilence or any deadly disease.
   2. The first three riders are not named. Here, the rider is Death. Death and Hell are the custodians of the bodies and souls of men.

             3.   One-fourth (¼) of the population will die because of war, famine, pestilence, and wild beasts.
             4.   In 1990, the world population was approximately five (5) billion people. If 5 billion will be the world population in the tribulation time and ¼ of the population dies, this means that 1 billion 250 million people will die. What an awful future lies ahead for the lost population of this world.

The Fifth Seal

V.   **THE SLAIN MARTYRS** – vs. 9-11
   a.   *"[9] And when He had opened the fifth seal, I saw under the altar the souls of them that were slain for the word of God, and for the testimony which they held: [10] And they cried with a loud voice, saying How long, O Lord, holy and true, dost thou not judge and avenge our blood on them that dwell on the earth? [11] And white robes were given unto every one of them; and it was said unto them, that they should rest yet for a little season, until their fellowservants also and their brethren, that should be killed as they were, should be fulfilled."* – Revelation 6:9-11
   b.   The Fifth (5th) Seal **(vs. 9)**
         1.   The slain martyrs are the saved of the tribulation day. They will pay with their lives.
               • The Reason for Their Death
                     ❖ For the Word of God **(vs. 9)**
                     ❖ For the Testimony which they held **(vs. 9)**
                     ❖ They were to wait a little season for vengeance until certain ***"fellowservants also and their brethren, that should be killed as they were, should be fulfilled."*** (vs. 11)

EPISODES OF THE END, THE REVELATION OF JESUS CHRIST

    2.   Verse 10 makes reference to them that dwell on the earth. It references those who live only for this earth and it's pursuits and pleasures, but have no interest in the eternal things of God.

    3.   There have been many martyrs, but according to verse 11, this is only the beginning. Many more are to follow, especially in the final scenes of this book of Revelation.

    4.   The world today is still in the spirit of rebellion. This is the reason for wars, famine, hardships, refugees, and many other things that fill the news of today.

The Sixth Seal

VI. **THE SHAKING** – vs. 12-17

    a.   *"[12] And I beheld when He had opened the sixth seal, and, lo, there was a great earthquake; and the sun became black as sackcloth of hair, and the moon became as blood; [13] And the stars of heaven fell unto the earth, even as a fig tree casteth her untimely figs, when she is shaken of a mighty wind. [14] And the heaven departed as a scroll when it is rolled together; and every mountain and island were moved out of their places. [15] and the kings of the earth, and the great men, and the rich men, and the chief captains, and the mighty men, and every bondman, and every free man, hid themselves in the dens and in the rocks of the mountains; [16] And said to the mountains and rocks, Fall on us, and hide us from the face of him that sitteth on the throne, and from the wrath of the Lamb: [17] For the great day of His wrath is come; and who shall be able to stand?"* – Revelation 6:12-17

    b.   <u>The Sixth (6th) Seal</u> **(vs. 12)**

        1.   Earthquakes are on the increase today. There will be a great one, for God is arising to

REVELATION—CHAPTER 6

"shake terribly the earth" **(Isaiah 2:19)** for man's sin.
2. There was a great earthquake when Christ bore our sin on the Cross.
   - **Matthew 27:51**
3. There was a great earthquake at His resurrection.
   - **Matthew 28:2**
4. Jesus prophesied about earthquakes.
   - **Luke 21:11**
5. John noted earthquakes in **Revelation 8:5** and **11:13-19**. But the greatest earthquake ever will take place after the seventh bowl of God's wrath is poured out in **Revelation 16:18**.
6. God is using nature to judge here.
   - God will blot out the sun, and the moon will become as blood. The first darkening of the sun and moon are *"before the great and terrible day of the Lord"* **(Acts 2:20 and Joel 2:31)**. The second darkening will be *"immediately after the tribulation"* **(Matthew 24:29)**. But, men in terror believe the end has come. When it does not, they grow hardened like Pharaoh, and we see them in **Revelation 19:19** boldly gathering to war against God whom here they dread.
   - Stars will fall like figs falling from a tree. Here stars refer to celestial bodies. With a black sun, a bloody moon, and falling stars, what a dark terror this will display. God be thanked. The Church will not pass through these Judgements. The Church will be in heaven with Christ.

c. The Shifting – **vs. 14**
   1. Here we see great turbulence in the heavens.
      - *"And the heaven departed as a scroll when it is rolled together; and every mountain and island were moved out of their places."* – Revelation 6:14

EPISODES OF THE END, THE REVELATION OF JESUS CHRIST

- This puts beyond question the fact that these Judgements are worldwide. Great fear now fills the earth.

d. <u>The Seeking</u> – **vs. 15-16**
    1. Men will seek the wrong things
- Mountains
- Rocks
  - ❖ They cannot speak
  - ❖ They cannot hear
  - ❖ They cannot save

    2. There are seven (7) kinds of men, all very much afraid
- Kings of the earth
- Great men
- Rich men
- Chief Captains
- Mighty men
- Bondman
- Free Man
  - ❖ People from every level of society are all filled with the fear of God's Judgements. They will try to hide in caves and among the rocks and mountains **(Isaiah 2:21)**, as if they could get away from God.
  - ❖ They will try to commit suicide and even ask the rocks and mountains to fall on them **(Hosea 10:8)**.

e. <u>The Solemn Day</u> – **vs. 17**
    1. John closes chapter 6 with these words:
- ***"For the great day of His wrath is come; and who shall be able to stand?"*** – NOT ONE.

Revelation – Chapter 7

Chapter seven is a parenthesis. It was put here for a reason. Its purpose is for the showing of God's mercy, *"in wrath remember mercy"* **(Habakkuk 3:2)**. Chapter seven is in two divisions.
- The first division covers verses 1-8, which have to do with the sealing of 144,000 from the twelve tribes of Israel.
- The second division covers verses 9-17, which is the great multitude of gentiles who are saved during the great tribulation.

The Saved of the Tribulation Period

I. **THE HOLDING BACK – vs. 1**
   a. *"And after these things I saw four angels standing on the four corners of the earth, holding the four winds of the earth, that the wind should not blow on the earth, nor on the sea, nor on any tree."* – **Revelation 7:1**
   b. The winds of Judgement have been blowing, but now the angels are holding them back in order that God may show mercy.
   c. Revelation Chapter 6 is interrupted by the scene of mercy in Revelation Chapter 7.
      1. Four (4) angels are executors of God
      2. Four (4) corners of the earth are the directions:
         - East
         - West
         - North
         - South
      3. Four (4) winds are the destruction or judgement
   d. Four (4) is the earth's number
   e. Angels are God's ministers **(Hebrews 1:7 and 14)**. They were active from the creation of man to the ascension of Christ.
   f. After the rapture of the Church, they will become prominent again. Even now, we do not know to what extent God is using them to protect His own and restrain the forces of wickedness.

EPISODES OF THE END, THE REVELATION OF JESUS CHRIST

- g. Angels seem to appear in times of crisis.
    1. Two (2) angels warned Sodom – **Genesis 19:1**
    2. Seven (7) angels with trumpets of judgement – **Revelation 8 and 9**
    3. One (1) mighty angel – **Revelation 10:1**
    4. One (1) angel that had power over fire – **Revelation 14:18**
    5. Seven (7) angels with the vials of the wrath of God upon the earth – **Revelation 16**
    6. One (1) angel in the sun – **Revelation 19:17**
    7. Angels coming with Christ at His second coming – **Matthew 25:31**

II. THE HURT NOT – vs. 2-3

- a. *" [2] And I saw another angel ascending from the east, having the seal of the living God: and he cried with a loud voice to the four angels, to whom it was given to hurt the earth and the sea, [3] Saying, Hurt not the earth, neither the sea, nor the trees, till we have sealed the servants of our God in their foreheads."* – Revelation 7:2-3
- b. The fifth angel has charge of sealing the 144,000.
    1. These are hurting days.
    2. God stops the storm to deal with the Jews.
    3. God never forgets the Jew. The Jew remains a distinct person right up until the Judgement. God has a future for the Jew **(Romans 9:4-5 and Romans 10 and 11)**. These Jews are proclaiming the message of God under Divine protection.

The Remnant out of Israel Sealed

III. THE HUNDRED FORTY FOUR THOUSAND – vs. 4-8

- a. *" [4] And I heard the number of them which were sealed: and there were sealed an hundred and forty and four thousand of all the tribes of tho children of Israel. [5] Of the tribe of Juda were sealed twelve thousand. Of the tribe of Reuben were sealed twelve thousand. Of the tribe of Gad were sealed twelve thousand. [6] Of the tribe of Aser were sealed twelve thousand. Of the tribe of Nepthalim were sealed twelve thousand. Of the tribe of Manasses were sealed twelve thousand. [7] Of the tribe of Simeon were sealed twelve thousand. Of the tribe of Levi were sealed twelve thousand. Of the tribe of Issachar were sealed twelve thousand. [8] Of the tribe of Zabulon were sealed twelve thousand. Of the tribe of Joseph were sealed twelve thousand. Of the tribe of Benjamin were sealed twelve thousand."* – **Revelation 7:4-8**

b. Many claim to be the 144,000 but the Bible plainly teaches that they are all Israelite Jews. The sealing takes place during the interval between the sixth and seventh seal. This falls within the first three and one-half years of the tribulation period. The numbering implies several things.

   1. It shows that the parties numbered are "the remnant" of Israel.
- According to God's promise, Israel was to be as innumerable as the dust **(Genesis 13:16 and Numbers 23:10)**.
- This is in accordance with Joel **(Joel 2:30-31)**, after he has predicted the signs in the sun and moon, which have preceded under the sixth seal, he adds *"and it shall come to pass that whosoever shall call on the Name of the Lord shall be delivered: for in mount Zion and in Jerusalem shall be deliverance, as the Lord hath said, and in the remnant whom the Lord shall call."* **(Joel 2:32)**.
- The 144,000 are the remnant marked as the Lord's signifying that the day of deliverance for Israel is at hand.
- These are the Jewish elect who are not deceived, when all others are led astray by

the wonders of the false Christ's **(Matthew 24:23-26)**.
2. It implies ownership.
- The Lord numbers His flock **(Jeremiah 33:13)**.
- The reference to flocks passing under the hand of one who counted them is a picture of the shepherd counting his flock at the end of the day to see that none was missing.
3. God numbered His elect in Elijah's day.
- ***"Yet I have left Me seven thousand in Israel..." – I Kings 19:18***
4. Numbering was also for war.
- Saul numbers the people **(I Samuel 11:8)**, before proceeding against Nahash (which means a serpent).
- He numbered them again before the war with the Philistines **(I Samuel 13:11-23)** and before the expedition against Amalek **(I Samuel 15:1-5)**.

c. God is preparing the sealed Israelites for service.
1. The meaning of their names:
- Juda (or Judah) – Praisers of God
  ❖ Praise stands for the great function of worship. Praise is glorifying to God, and no one ever glorified Him more in service than Christ did. Judah is the ruling tribe. Jesus is of this tribe, and is called the Lion of the tribe of Judah **(Revelation 5:5)**. David is from this tribe also **(Matthew 1:1-17)**.
- Reuben – Son seen; Son of vision
  ❖ Reuben was the first born of Jacob and Leah. As the first born he was entitled to three portions above his brethren, in the priesthood, the birthright, and the kingdom. But all three were forfeited and given to others.
  ❖ Reuben lost all the honors that should have been his because of his adulterous act with Bilhah, his father's

concubine. The sin of adultery brought a curse upon him **(Genesis 35:22, I Chronicles 5:1-2,** see birthright **Deuteronomy 21:15-17)**.
- Gad – A company; A troop
  - ❖ God enabled to frustrate and defeat his foes **(I Chronicles 5:18-22)**.
- Aser – Blessed One
  - ❖ His blessing given by Jacob on his deathbed is thus worded *"out of Aser (Asher) his bread shall be fat, and he shall yield royal dainties"* **(Genesis 49:20)**.
  - ❖ Aser was the tribe of rich pastures. Aser dwelt in the midst of plenty and being willing to share what he had with his brethren.
- Nepthalim – Wrestling with
  - ❖ Rachel gave him this name because she had wrestled in prayer for God's favor and blessing **(Genesis 30:8)**.
- Manasseh – Causing forgetfulness
  - ❖ That is forgetting Joseph's trials in Egypt **(Genesis 41:51)**.
  - ❖ Manasseh, the elder son of Joseph, was born in Egypt and was half-Hebrew and half-Egyptian. Joseph was caused to forget his toil and trouble in Egypt and even his father's house. Evidently, the bitter memories of Joseph's past experiences would literally flee from his mind.
- Simeon – Hearing and Obeying
  - ❖ Simeon and Levi are taken together because their records are so similar. They acted together in the episode involving the avenging of Dinah their sister **(Genesis 34:1-31)**.
  - ❖ They were men of:
    1. Cruelty – **Genesis 49:5**
    2. Anger – **Genesis 49:6**

3. Murders – slew and man – **Genesis 49:6**
4. Self Will – **Genesis 49:6**
5. Cursed – **Genesis 49:7**
   - *"...I will divide them in Jacob, and scatter them in Israel."* **(Genesis 49:7)**. This was fulfilled in that Simeon, as the smallest tribe, was not given a separate portion of land but a part of Judah with which it appears to have joined **(Joshua 19:1, 21:9; I Chronicles 4:24-38)**. Levi had no inheritance in Israel but was given scattered cities among the tribes **(Joshua 13:33, 21:1-45)**.

- Levi – Cleaving to
  - ❖ Simeon and Levi were brothers, even though they failed and sinned grievously, and judgement was pronounced upon them, and they did not live up to the meaning of their names. Though divided and scattered, they were not cut off from the Promised Land. But, theirs was not the abundant entrance of others, yet they were privileged to enter.
  - ❖ Their names are written on two (2) of the gates of the New Jerusalem with the other ten (10) tribes **(Revelation 21:12)**. In this we see the grace and mercy of God.
- Issachar – A reward
  - ❖ The birth of Issachar was regarded by his mother as kind of payment from the hand of God; "God hath given me my hire" **(Genesis 30:18)**.
  - ❖ Issachar is described as a strong ass (donkey). In the Bible, the donkey was

viewed as an admirably, durable, and useful animal. It was used extensively to carry its owner or do various types of hard work. The impression given is of a tribe with unrealized potential. The land and experience had similarities with those of Zebulon, but they seem to have made less of their opportunities.

- Zebulon – A home and dwelling place
  - ❖ Zebulon became the earthly habitation for the Lord of Glory as prophesied by Isaiah **(Isaiah 9:1-7).** Zebulon is used as God's dwelling in the temple **(II Chronicles 6:2)** and of a haven **(Isaiah 63:15)**. The borders of Zebulon's tribe would touch the sea as Jacob predicted in **Genesis 49:13**. This means a haven (a cove) of ships. God uses all kinds of business for His glory.
- Joseph – Adding
  - ❖ The meaning of Joseph's name directs us to fruitful increase as the outcome of genuine discipleship. Joseph was ever true to the instruction he received and went forth in confidence, increasing in knowledge and fruitfulness.
- Benjamin – Son of my right hand
  - ❖ A figure suggesting heirship. Benjamin was the only one of the 12 sons of Jacob born in Israel **(Genesis 35:16-20)**. Rachel died while giving birth to Benjamin. She called him Ben-oni meaning son of sorrow, a type of the suffering of Christ. But, to his father he was the son of my right hand.
  - ❖ Paul tells us that Christ *"sitteth at the right hand of God"* **(Colossians 3:1)**.
  - ❖ **Mark 16:19 says *"He was received up in Heaven and sat on the right hand of God."*** At God's right hand, it is a place of:

| | | 1. | Exaltation of Jesus – **Philippians 2:9-11** |
| | | 2. | Intercession of Jesus – **Hebrews 7:25** |

> ❖ Benjamin was a type of Christ as Christ is God's Son seated at His right hand.

    d.   The 144,000 is a remnant of Jewish believers, set apart and sealed by God, to be a testimony of God's mercy during the time of tribulation and judgement.

    e.   The tribes of Dan and Ephraim are omitted in this enumeration. Levi and Joseph are inserted in their place. The reason for this seems quite clear. Moses warned Israel (man, woman, family, or tribe) against introducing idolatry into their worship **(Deuteronomy 29:18-26)**. Dan and Ephraim were the first of the tribes to introduce idol worship in Israel **(Judges 18)**. Afterward Jeroboam made the golden calves and set one of them in the tribe of Dan **(I Kings 11:26; 12:28-30)**. The prophet Hosea chastised Ephraim for idolatry **(Hosea 4:17)**, spiritual unfaithfulness **(Hosea 8:9-10)**, and relationships with heathen nations **(Hosea 12:1)**. However Dan and Ephraim will have an important place in the millennial Kingdom of Christ and will worship God there **(Ezekiel 48:1-7)**. In Dan and Ephraim we see *"but where sin abounded, grace did much more abound"* **(Romans 5:20)**.

The Gentiles Who Are to be Saved During the Great Tribulation

IV.   THE HARVEST – vs. 9

    a.   *"After this I beheld, and, lo, a great multitude, which no man could number, of all nations, and kindreds, and people, and tongues, stood before the throne, and before the Lamb, clothed in white robes, and palms in their hands:"* – Revelation 7:9

    b.   *"...a great multitude which no man could number"*; they are Gentiles who are saved during the great tribulation.

c. God knows the number, who they are, and where they are.

V. **THE HOLY PEOPLE** – vs. 9
   a. *"...clothed in white robes..."* – **Revelation 7:9**
   b. White robes speak of God's righteousness clothed in perfection.
   c. *"For He hath made Him to be sin for us, who knew no sin; that we might be made the righteousness of God in Him." – II Corinthians 5:21*

VI. **THE HAPPY PEOPLE** – vs. 9-12
   a. *"[9]...and palms in their hands:...[10] And cried with a loud voice, saying Salvation to our God which sitteth upon the throne, and unto the Lamb. [11] And all the angels stood round about the throne, and about the elders and the four beasts, and fell before the throne on their faces and worshipped God, [12] Saying, Amen: Blessing and glory, and wisdom, and thanksgiving, and honour, and power, and might, be unto our God for ever, and ever. Amen." – Revelation 7:9-12*
   b. Palms in their hands are an expression of joy.
   c. They are praising God for salvation (**vs. 10**).
   d. This is a portrait of true worship (**vs. 11-12**).

VII. **THE HARDSHIP** – vs. 13-16
   a. *" [13] And one of the elders answered, saying unto me, What are these which are arrayed in white robes? And whence came they? [14] And I said unto him, Sir, thou knowest. And he said to me, These are they which came out of great tribulation, and have washed their robes, and made them white in the blood of the Lamb. [15] Therefore are they before the throne of God, and serve Him day and night in His temple: and He that sitteth on the throne shall dwell among them. [16] They shall hunger no more, neither thirst any more; neither*

shall the sun light on them, nor any heat." – Revelation 7:13-16
- b. The great tribulation
  1. The silence of the seer – **vs. 13-14**
     - *"And one of the elders answered, saying unto me, What are these which are arrayed in white robes? And whence came they? [14] And I said unto him, <u>Sir, thou knowest</u>. And he said to me, These are they which came out of great tribulation, ..."*
  2. The surety of their salvation – **vs. 14**
     - *"...the blood of the Lamb."*
  3. The service of the saints – **vs. 15**
     - *"...serve Him day and night..."*
  4. Their suffering ended – **vs. 16**
     - *"They shall hunger no more, neither thirst any more; neither shall the sun light on them, nor any heat."*
     - Earthly trials are over.
     - There is no discomfort in Heaven.
     - There is no need for anything in Heaven.

VIII. THEIR HOME – vs. 17
- a. *"For the Lamb which is in the midst of the throne shall feed them, and shall lead them unto living fountains of waters: and God shall wipe away all tears from their eyes."* – Revelation 7:17
- b. *"...lead them unto living fountains of waters..."* – Notice that waters is plural meaning
  1. The water of salvation
  2. The water of the Holy Spirit
  3. The water of the Word
- c. *"...God shall wipe away all tears from their eyes."*
  1. There will be no tears in Heaven.
  2. There will be nothing to cry about.
  3. Home at last, "Alleluias".

Revelation – Chapter 8

The Calm Before the Storm

The Seventh Seal

I. **THE SILENCE IN HEAVEN – vs. 1**
   a. ***"And when He had opened the seventh seal, there was silence in heaven about the space of half an hour." – Revelation 8:1***
   b. This is the lull before the storm. So, there is a calm of silence before this future storm of judgement.
      1. The Seventh (7th) Seal – **vs. 1**
- Out of this seal comes a new set of judgements.
- The seven trumpets
  ❖ The steps of God, from mercy to judgement are always slow, reluctant, and measured. This is God's strange work. A long forbearing God is about to visit strokes of judgement upon men.

      2. The Silence – **vs. 1**
- The silence is because of the solemn purpose of judgement

      3. The Space of Half an Hour – **vs. 1**
- It is a time of preparation.
  ❖ This is so that the prayers of the saints may be offered to the Lord. The prayers of all the saints are sent up before God **(vs. 3-5)**.
- It is a time of reflection.
  ❖ Attentive consideration; to think seriously.
- Pause before the storm

The Seven Trumpets

II. THE SEVEN ANGELS AND THE SEVEN TRUMPETS – vs. 2

a. *"And I saw the seven angels which stood before God; and to them were given seven trumpets."* – **Revelation 8:2**

b. The angels are God's executors, each holding a trumpet. In the Bible, trumpets are used in various ways.
   1. A summons to worship
      - **Numbers 10:3-7**
      - **I Chronicles 16:37 and 42**
   2. Warfare
      - **Numbers 10:5-9**
   3. The idea of the trumpet originated with God.
      - **Numbers 10:1-2**
      - The trumpet was made of silver, which is a type of redemption. God originated redemption.
      - It speaks of testimony.
   4. Priests were the only ones qualified to blow the trumpets.
      - **Number 10:8**
   5. There were different sounds for each occasion.
      - **Numbers 10:1-10**
      - *"For if the trumpet give an uncertain sound, who shall prepare himself to the battle?"* – **I Corinthians 14:8**

III. THE SAVIOR – vs. 3-5

a. *"[3] And another angel came and stood at the altar, having a golden censer; and there was given unto him much incense, that he should offer it with the prayers of all saints upon the golden altar which was before the throne. [4] And the smoke of the incense which came with the prayers of the saints, ascended up before God out of the angel's hand. [5] And the angel took the censer, and filled it with fire of the altar, and cast it into the earth: and there were voices, and thunderings, and lightnings, and an earthquake."* – **Revelation 8:3-5**

b. ***"Another angel"***, I believe is Christ Himself. The reference here is to the altar of burnt offerings **(Leviticus 9:24)**. The fire miraculously kindled by God, *"And there came a fire out from before the Lord, and consumed upon the altar the burnt-offering and the fat: ..."*

c. The burnt offering typifying Christ's mediatorial work.
   1. In verses 3 through 5, we have:
      - The Priestly Work of Christ – **vs. 3**
         - *"...and there was given unto him much incense, that he should offer it with the prayers of all saints upon the golden altar which was before the throne."* – (vs. 3)
      - The Prayers of the Saints – **vs. 4**
         - *"...the prayers of the saints, ascended up before God..."* – (vs. 4)
         - God is hearing the prayers of the tribulation saints, which are going up to Him.
         - Censer was used yearly on the Great Day of Atonement **(Leviticus 16)**.
         - It was made of Gold **(Hebrews 9:4)** and used to carry fire from off the altar **(Leviticus 16:12)**.
         - The incense represents Christ's person and work on Calvary. Christ's life and work make our prayers effective **(Ephesians 5:2)**.
      - The Power of Prayer – **vs. 5**
         - After prayer ascends **(vs. 4)**, judgement descends **(vs. 5)**.
         - The angel fills his censer with fire from off the brazen altar of judgement. He casts it into the earth and then follows a token of judgement, *"...voices, and thunderings, and lightnings, and an earthquake."*, a foretaste of the trumpet judgements to follow.

EPISODES OF THE END, THE REVELATION OF JESUS CHRIST

IV. **THE SUMMONS** – vs. 6
    a. *"And the seven angels which had the seven trumpets prepared themselves to sound." –* **Revelation 8:6**
    b. Heaven itself is now ready to execute judgement upon the wicked world as set forth in the first five verses of this chapter. The angels now prepare to inflict the penalty **(vs. 6)**.

> The First through the Fourth Trumpet

V. **THE STORM BREAKS FORTH** – vs. 7-13
    a. *" [7] The first angel sounded, and there followed hail and fire mingled with blood, and they were cast upon the earth: and the third part of trees was burnt up, and all green grass was burnt up. [8] And the second angel sounded, and as it were a great mountain burning with fire was cast into the sea: and the third part of the sea became blood: [9] And the third part of the creatures which were in the sea, and had life, died; and the third part of the ships were destroyed. [10] And the third angel sounded, and there fell a great star from heaven, burning as it were a lamp, and it fell upon the third part of the rivers, and upon the foundations of waters. [11] And the name of the star is called Wormwood: and the third part of the waters became wormwood; and many men died of the waters, because they were made bitter. [12] And the fourth angel sounded, and the third part of the sun was smitten, and the third part of the moon, and the third part of the stars; so as the third part of them was darkened, and the day shone not for a third part of it, and the night likewise. [13] And I beheld, and heard an angel flying through the midst of heaven, saying with a loud voice, "woe, woe, woe to the inhabiters of the earth by reason of the other voices of the trumpet*

of the three angels, which are yet to sound!" – **Revelation 8:7-13**

- b. The First Trumpet – **vs. 7**
    1. One third (1/3) of all trees and all pastureland burned up. No wonder a little later, the anti-Christ launches the greatest rationing system ever schemed by man.
- c. The Second Trumpet – **vs. 8**
    1. The third part of the sea became blood. The third part of the creatures in the sea died. The third part of the ships destroyed. Another reason for a rationing system.
- d. The Third Trumpet – **vs. 10-11**
    1. Judgement falls upon fresh water supply of the whole earth. One third of the water will be unfit to drink and many men will die.
- e. The Fourth Trumpet – **vs. 12**
    1. Certain astronomical effects by a cause not stated. The third part of the Sun, Moon, and Stars are darkened depriving the earth of normal light. This will affect vegetation, health, and vocation.
    2. There is no word said about men repenting and asking God for mercy.

There are three (3) trumpets to come, heralded by three woes. Men are no better: but they are warned. **(vs. 13)**

Revelation – Chapter 9

Invaded By Hordes From Another World

The Fifth Trumpet – The First Woe

I. **THE LOUD SOUND – vs. 1**
- a. *"And the fifth angel sounded, and I saw a star fall from heaven unto the earth: and to Him was given the key of the bottomless pit."* – Revelation 9:1
- b. The word "sounded" means to sound a blast, make a great noise.
- c. The "star" that fell from heaven is a person. He is called "him" and is the angel custodian of the pit.
- d. Bible Scholars are not in agreement to who this star is. Some say it is
    1. Satan
    2. A Demon
    3. An Evil Angel

    I personally believe He is the same one who binds Satan in **Revelation 20:1-2**. I believe this is Christ Himself. He has the keys of hell and death **(Revelation 1:18)**.

II. **THE LOW PIT – vs. 2**
- a. *"And He opened the bottomless pit; and there arose a smoke out of the pit, as the smoke of a great furnace; and the sun and the air were darkened by reason of the smoke of the pit."* – Revelation 9:2
- b. This is the fearful prison of evil and unruly spirits, and has its lid somewhere on the surface of the earth.
- c. The demons at Gadara besought Christ not to send them into the deep (or the pit). They had rather enter into the bodies of the swine **(Mark 5:1-17)**.
- d. The demons dread the pit and shun it knowing that it is their future home.

- e. Satan now has millions of fallen angels and demons to work for him. But, there is a dark horrible pit full of strange and evil beings that is closed to protect mankind from their fearful torment.
- f. When the bottomless pit was open, **"there arose a smoke out of the pit, as the smoke of a great furnace"**, so thick that the sun and the air were darkened **(vs. 2)**. Throughout Revelation, smoke is associated with judgement, doom, and torment.

III. THE LOCUSTS – vs. 3-4

- a. **"[3] And there came out of the smoke locusts upon the earth: and unto them was given power, as the scorpions of the earth have power. [4] And it was commanded them that they should not hurt the grass of the earth, neither any green things, neither any tree; but only those men which have not the seal of God in their foreheads."**- Revelation 9:3-4
- b. Regular locusts may lie dormant for seventeen (17) years and come forth to bring destruction to vegetation. But here are demonic locusts that have been locked up for ages, now turned loose with a commission to hurt no green thing, but **"only those men which have not the seal of God in their foreheads"** (vs. 4).

IV. THE LINGERING – vs. 5

- a. **"And to them it was given that they should not kill them, but that they should be tormented five months: and their torment was as the torment of a scorpion, when he striketh a man."** – Revelation 9:5
- b. What mercy God shows to our present age that these creatures are locked up. And what torment the future holds for those who reject God's mercy.

V. THE LAMENTATION – vs. 6

- a. ***"And in those days shall men seek death, and shall not find it; and shall desire to die, and death shall flee from them."* – Revelation 9:6**
- b. Though seldom fatal, the sting of a scorpion is one of the most painful stings known. The venom seems to set the veins and nervous system on fire, lasting for several days.
- c. One day in the future, these creatures of sorrow will be turned loose upon mankind and men will twist in pain and agony.
- d. Think of eternal hell with all of these creatures as companions, and yet, men build on the very edge of hell and boast of their great wisdom. The torment will last for five (5) months. What an awful cry in that day.
- e. There will not be any suicides or funerals.
- f. But the day is not far in the future when men will welcome death and court disaster. Just what would happen if a man were to hold a shot gun to his head or sink himself in a lake, we do not know. Suicide will not bring relief, for death shall flee from him. It may be that these creatures will be able, in some way, to prevent suicide as part of their torment.

VI. THE LOCUST'S DESCRIPTION – vs. 7-10

- a. ***"[7] And the shapes of the locusts were like unto horses prepared unto battle; and on their heads were as it were crowns like gold, and their faces were as the faces of men. [8] And they had hair as the hair of women, and their teeth were as the teeth of lions. [9] And they had breastplates, as it were breastplates of iron; and the sound of their wings was as the sound of chariots of many horses running to battle. [10] And they had tails like unto scorpions, and there were stings in their tails: and their power was to hurt men five months."* – Revelation 9:7-10**
- b. *"...like unto horses..."* (vs. 7)
  1. Signifying war
- c. *"...on their heads were as it were crowns like gold..."* (vs. 7)

                1. Make believe sovereignty – Imitator of real sovereignty
- d. *"...their faces were as the faces of men..."* (vs. 7)
  1. Intelligence
- e. *"...they had hair as the hair of women..."* (vs. 8)
  1. Suggests something horrible, yet seductive and attractive about them
- f. *"...their teeth were as the teeth of lions..."* (vs. 8)
  1. Destruction
- g. *"...they had breastplates, as it were breastplates of iron..."* (vs. 9)
  1. Immune from personal destruction – they show no pity
- h. *"...their wings was as the sound of chariots of many horses running to battle..."* (vs. 9)
  1. They are inescapable. They travel and strike terror and fear in victims.
- i. *"...there were stings in their tails..."* (vs. 10)
  1. They are injurious and had power to hurt men for five (5) months.

VIII. THE LEADER OF THE LOCUSTS – vs. 11

- a. *"And they had a king over them, which is the angel of the bottomless pit, whose name in Hebrew tongue is Abaddon, but in the Greek tongue hath his name Apollyon."* – Revelation 9:11
- b. The name of the angel of the bottomless pit in Hebrew is Abaddon and in Greek is Apollyon. Both mean destroyer.
- c. I believe the angel of the bottomless pit is Satan himself. He is a deceiver, a thief, a murderer, and destroyer of the souls of men.
- d. The followers of Satan do not build, but destroy.

The Great Army of Horsemen

The Sixth Trumpet

I. **THE BLAST** – vs. 13
   a.   *"And the sixth angel sounded, and I heard a voice from the four horns of the golden altar which is before God,"* – Revelation 9:13
   b.   In **Revelation 8:3**, the altar is the scene of the offering of incense of the prayers of the saints. Here in **Revelation 9:13**, this is the final mention of the altar in Revelation. This is judgement like the preceding and is partially an answer to the prayer of the persecuted saint on the earth.

II. **THE BOUND ANGELS** – vs. 14-16
   a.   *"[14] Saying to the sixth angel which had the trumpet, Loose the four angels which are bound in the great river Euphrates. [15] And the four angels were loosed, which were prepared for an hour, and a day, and a month, and a year, for to slay the third part of men. [16] And the number of the army of the horsemen were two hundred thousand thousand: and I heard the number of them."* – Revelation 9:14-16
   b.   These are evil angels, in the fact that they are bound and are leaders of a demon army of two hundred million (200,000,000). We are not told why they are bound in this particular region of the world. The Euphrates was one of the four (4) rivers, which flowed out of the Garden of Eden **(Genesis 2:10-14)**.
       1.   The Garden of Eden was somewhere in this region.
       2.   The sin of man began here. **(Genesis 3)**
       3.   The first murder was committed here. **(Genesis 4)**
       4.   The flood began here. **(Genesis 7)**
       5.   The tower of Babel, the first organized rebellion against God, began here. **(Genesis 11)**
   c.   Even now, the four (4) angels are being prepared for a specific time to loose the demon army of 200,000,000. Their mission is to slay the third part of men.

REVELATION—CHAPTER 9

III. THE BRIMSTONE – vs. 17-19
a. *"[17] And thus I saw the horses in the vision, and them that sat on them, having breastplates of fire, and of jacinth, and brimstone: and the heads of the horses were as the heads of lions: and out of their mouths issued fire and smoke and brimstone. [18] By these three was the third part of men killed, by the fire, and by the smoke, and by the brimstone, which issued out of their mouths. [19] For their power is in their mouth, and their tails: for their tails were like unto serpents, and had heads, and with them they do hurt."* – Revelation 9:17-19
b. Their weapons
  1. Fire
  2. Brimstone
  3. Smoke
  4. Their Mouth
  5. Their Tails

IV. THE BLINDNESS – vs. 20-21
a. *"[20] And the rest of the men which were not killed by these plagues yet repented not of the works of their hands, that thy should not worship devils, and idols of gold, and silver, and brass, and stone, and of wood: which neither can see, nor hear, nor walk: [21] Neither repented they of their murders, nor of their sorceries, nor of their fornication, nor of their thefts."* – Revelation 9:20-21
b. They worshipped
  1. Devils or Demons
  2. Idols
  3. Gold
  4. Silver
  5. Brass
  6. Stone
  7. Wood
  8. *"...which neither can see, nor hear, nor walk..."* (vs. 20)
c. The World Waxes Worse

EPISODES OF THE END, THE REVELATION OF JESUS CHRIST

1. ***"Neither repented they of their..."*** **(vs. 21)**
   - Murders
     - ❖ Abortion of unborn babies
     - ❖ Murders of mankind
   - Sorceries
     - ❖ To be enchanted with drugs
   - Fornication
     - ❖ A hint that marriage is done away with
   - Thefts
     - ❖ Our day abounds in dishonesty, deceit, and theft
2. This is abounding iniquity. The let down in morals is gradual. So here, the characteristic of the age has been a general let down in morals.
3. Today mankind is becoming more
   - Selfish – lovers of themselves
   - Covetous
   - Boaster
   - Proud
   - Blasphemers
   - Disobedient
   - Unthankful
   - Unholy
   - Without Natural Affection
   - Trucebreakers
   - False Accusers
   - Incontinent
   - Fierce
   - Despisers of those that are good
   - Traitors
   - Heady
   - Highminded
   - Lovers of pleasure more than lovers of God
     - ❖ **II Timothy 3:2-4**
     - ❖ As in the days of Noah, so will these things be in the day of Christ's return **(Matthew 24:37-39).**
     - ❖ How blind are those who comfort themselves by saying this world is getting better.

❖ *"But evil men and seducers shall wax worse and worse, deceiving and being deceived."* – II Timothy 3:13

Revelation – Chapter 10

The events in Chapter 10:1 through Chapter 11:14 lie between the sounds of the sixth (6th) trumpet and the seventh (7th) trumpet.

The Mighty Angel and the Little Book

I. **THE CHRIST** – vs. 1
    a. *"And I saw another mighty angel come down from heaven, clothed with a cloud: and a rainbow was upon His head, and His face was as it were the sun, and His feet as pillars of fire:"* – **Revelation 10:1**
    b. Some believe this to be just a mighty angel. I believe it to be none other than Christ Himself.
    c. He stands with one foot on the sea and one on the earth signifying universal authority **(vs. 2)**.
        1. *"The earth is the Lord's and the fulness thereof; the world, and they that dwell therein."* – **Psalm 24:1**
    d. The Coming Down – **vs. 1**
        1. He came down the first time to die on the cross to save us from our sins **(Matthew 1:21)**.
        2. He is coming down the second time to judge the world **(Acts 17:31)**.
    e. Clothed with a Cloud – **vs. 1**
        1. *"...cloud..."* – a public sign of His majesty
        2. *"...rainbow..."* – ancient token of Divine goodness **(Genesis 9:11-17)**
           • God's remembrance of mercy
        3. *"...face as it were sun..."* – this is a powerful reminder of His holiness and His glory.
        4. *"...feet as pillars of fire..."* – stability and firmness

II. **THE CONSEQUENCES** – vs. 2

- a. ***"And He had in His hand a little book open: and He set His right foot upon the sea, and His left foot on the earth," – Revelation 10:2***
- b. The little book is the same as in Revelation chapter 5. It is the title deed to the earth. It contains the wrath of the great tribulation. It opens what Daniel was told to seal **(Daniel 12:4)** to the time of the end. All unfulfilled prophecies are now revealed and must come to pass.
  1. Right foot upon the sea – Rebellious nations **(Isaiah 57:20)**
  2. Left foot upon the earth – Civilized portion of the earth

III. THE CRY – vs. 3
- a. ***"And cried with a loud voice, as when a lion roareth: and when he had cried, seven thunders uttered their voices." – Revelation 10:3***
- b. The loud cry is heard over all the earth. Christ declares Himself to rule and His intention of doing so.
  1. *"...lion roareth..."* – judgement coming
  2. *"...seven thunders..."* – judgement completed
- c. Seven is God's number of completion.
- d. The earth, which belongs to God by right of creation and redemption, is about to be claimed by force and arms by God.

IV. THE CLOSED BOOK – vs. 4
- a. ***"And when the seven thunders had uttered their voices, I was about to write: and I heard a voice from heaven saying unto me, Seal up those things which the seven thunders uttered, and write them not." – Revelation 10:4***
- b. The seven (7) thunders are the only part of Revelation, which has been sealed. The rest God says *"...Seal not the sayings of the prophecy of this book: for the time is at hand."* (Revelation 22:10)
- c. There is a perfect, mighty, secret operation of God's power in judgement as well as salvation

(Deuteronomy 29:29). Probably, some day we will understand this sealed message. John did. He was about to write everything that God revealed to him, but it was not written down.

V. THE CREATOR – vs. 5-6

a. *"[5] And the angel which I saw stand upon the sea and upon the earth lifted up his hand to heaven, [6] And sware by him that liveth for ever and ever, who created heaven, and the things that therein are, and the earth, and the things that therein are, and the sea, and the things which are therein, that there should be time no longer."* – **Revelation 10:5-6**

b. The lifted hand toward heaven speaks of the Lord having total possession.

c. He is the creator of all things in heaven and earth.

1. *"For by Him were all things created, that are in heaven, and that are in earth, visible and invisible, whether they be thrones, or dominions, or principalities, or powers: all things were created by Him and for Him."* – **Colossians 1:16**

2. *"...time no longer"* simply means that time should no longer intervene or delay. The time is now about to be fulfilled and the execution of the final vengeance should no longer be delayed.

3. Man's day is drawing to an end. It will close in sharp and severe judgement.

4. When Christ returns, then will He ask, and the Father will give Him the kingdom over which He will rule from His own throne and which, though centered in Jerusalem, will include the ends of the earth.

5. As for Christ, the throne is His. The nations are His inheritance **(Psalm 2:8)**.

REVELATION—CHAPTER 10

VI. THE COMPLETED MYSTERY – vs. 7
a. *"But in the days of the voice of the seventh angel, when he shall begin to sound, the mystery of God should be finished as he hath declared to his servants the prophets." –* Revelation 10:7
b. Now Christ is about to wrest the government of this world from Satan and put him in the bottomless pit for one thousand (1,000) years, and rule and reign in power and great glory.
c. *"But in the days..."* indicating a progressive time element, in which the succeeding and seventh angel shall sound forth final judgement of woes and suffering.
d. *"...the mystery of God should be finished..."* -
  1. The mystery of God's long tolerance of evil will be finished.
  2. The mystery of retribution
  3. The mystery of predestination
  4. The mystery of the great struggle between light and darkness and good and evil.
  5. That which we do not understand now, all will be explained then.

VII. THE LITTLE BOOK – vs. 8-10
a. *"[8] And the voice which I heard from heaven spake unto me again, and said, Go and take the little book which is open in the hand of the angel which standeth upon the sea and upon the earth. [9] And I went unto the angel, and said unto him, Give me the little book. And he said unto me, Take it, and eat it up; and it shall make thy belly bitter, but it shall be in thy mouth sweet as honey. [10] And I took the little book out of the angel's hand, and ate it up; and it was in my mouth sweet as honey: and as soon as I had eaten it, my belly was bitter." –* Revelation 10:8-10
b. The little book is the Word of God.
  1. *"sweet"*
     - *"How sweet are thy words unto my taste! Yea sweeter than honey to my mouth!" –* Psalm 119:103

- The future will be glorious and sweet for the saved.
2. ***"bitter"***
    - The future will be weeping for the sinner; the little book included the Good News of creation's coming deliverance, but also included the doom of the wicked.
        - ❖ The bread of God
            - ♦ Jesus is the true bread from heaven **(John 6:32)**.
            - ♦ Jesus is the bread of God **(John 6:33)**.
            - ♦ Jesus is the bread of life **(John 6:35)**.
            - ♦ ***"Man shall not live by bread alone, but by every word that proceedeth out of the mouth of God."*** – **Matthew 4:4**

VIII. THE BURDEN – vs. 11
    a.   ***"And he said unto me, Thou must prophesy again before many people, and nations, and tongues, and kings."*** – **Revelation 10:11**
    b.   *"...must prophesy again..."*
        1. The words "people", "nations", and "kings" reminds us much of the judgement in Psalm 2 where each are all mentioned.
        2. ***"[1] Why do the heathen rage, and the people imagine a vain thing? [2] The kings of the earth set themselves, and the rulers take counsel together, against the Lord, and against his anointed, saying, [3] Let us break their bands asunder, and cast away their cords from us."*** – **Psalms 2:1-3**
        3. It is to this company of raging nations, vain imagining people, and confederated kings that John must prophecy too. But the revolt will be, that in the end time ***"Thou shalt break them with a rod of iron; thou shalt dash them in pieces like a potter's vessel."*** – **Psalm 2:9**

4. This is fulfilled in **Revelation 19:15** where we read *"And out of his mouth goeth a sharp sword, that with it he should smite the nations: and he shall rule them with a rod of iron: and he treadeth the winepress of the fierceness and wrath of Almighty God."*

Revelation – Chapter 11

The Times of the Gentiles to End in Forty-two Months

I. **THE TEMPLE** – vs. 1
    a. *"And there was given me a reed like unto a rod: and the angel stood, saying, Rise, and measure the temple of God, and the altar, and them that worship therein."* – **Revelation 11:1**
    b. There have been at least three (3) temples built in Jerusalem.
        1. Solomon's temple **(I Kings 8)**
            • It was destroyed by Nebuchadnezzar **(II Kings 24 and 25)**
        2. Zerubbabel's temple **(Ezra 3)**
            • It was destroyed by Antiochus Epiphanes in 168 BC.
        3. Herod's temple **(John 2:20)**
            • It was destroyed by the Roman General, Titus, in 70 AD.
    c. The temple in this present age is the Church – **Ephesians 2:19-22**
    d. In **Revelation 11:1**, the temple will be built in the first 3½ years of the tribulation. The Jews will be under the protection of the anti-Christ. During that time, they will be able to build the temple.
    e. The Jews will make a covenant with the anti-Christ **(Daniel 9:27)**.
    f. The temple will be built in Jerusalem **(Daniel 9:24)**.
    g. The anti-Christ will appear and claim to be God, and the right to be worshipped as God **(II Thessalonians 2:4)**. This is the abomination of desolation **(Daniel 9:27 and Matthew 24:15)**.
    h. The temple reveals man as he really is, an earthbound creature.

II. **THE TREADING** – vs. 2

      a.   *"But the court which is without the temple leave out, and measure it not; for it is given unto the Gentiles: and the holy city shall they tread under foot forty and two months."* – **Revelation 11:2**
      b.   *"...the holy city shall they tread under foot..."* – **vs. 2**
            1.   This shows the blindness of the Gentiles going on in their rebellion against God.
            2.   *"Why do the heathen rage,..."* – **Psalms 2:1**
      c.   The Time – **vs. 2**
            1.   42 months (or 3½ years), that is, until the end of the tribulation when Christ returns – **Matthew 24:29-31**.

The Two Witnesses to Prophesy Forty Two Months

III.   <u>THE TWO WITNESSES</u> – vs. 3-12
      a.   *"[3] And I will give power unto my two witnesses, and they shall prophesy a thousand two hundred and threescore days, clothed in sackcloth. [4] These are the two olive trees, and the two candlesticks standing before the God of the earth. [5] And if any man will hurt them, fire proceedeth out of their mouth, and devoureth their enemies: and if any man will hurt them, he must in this manner be killed. [6] These have power to shut heaven, that it rain not in the days of their prophecy: and have power over waters to turn them to blood, and to smite the earth with all plagues, as often as they will. [7] And when they shall have finished their testimony, the beast that ascendeth out of the bottomless pit shall make war against them, and shall overcome them, and kill them. [8] And their dead bodies shall lie in the street of the great city, which spiritually is called Sodom and Egypt, where also our Lord was crucified. [9] And they of the people and kindreds and tongues and nations shall see their dead bodies three days and an half, and shall not suffer their dead bodies to be put in graves. [10] And*

they that dwell upon the earth shall rejoice over them, and make merry, and shall send gifts one to another; because these two prophets tormented them that dwelt on the earth. [11] And after three days and an half the spirit of life from God entered into them, and they stood upon their feet: and great fear fell upon them which saw them. [12] And they heard a great voice from heaven saying unto them, Come up hither. And they ascended up to heaven in a cloud; and their enemies beheld them." – Revelation 11:3-12

b. They have power – **vs. 3**
   1. *"...I will give power unto my two witnesses..."* **(vs. 3)**
c. They have protected power – **vs. 5**
d. They have plague power – **vs. 6**
e. Their testimony – **vs. 7**
f. Their total sacrifice – **vs. 7-8**
   1. Martyrdom
   2. *"...their dead bodies shall lie in the street of the great city..."* for 3½ days. **(vs. 8-9)**
g. There have been several suggestions as to the identity of these two (2) powerful preachers.
   1. Elijah and Enoch
   2. Elijah and John the Baptist
   3. Elijah and Moses
- I do not know who the two witnesses are, but the evidence seems to me, to identify them as being Elijah and Moses. A number of scholars believe the two witnesses will not be figures from the past but will exhibit a ministry similar to Elijah's and Moses'. This position has some merit because the text does not identify the two witnesses by name. If they are from the past, Elijah and Moses seem to be the best candidates as far as my understanding of this.
- The witnesses are described as *"two olive trees and the two candlesticks standing before the God of the earth"*. **(vs. 4)** Their mission is similar to that of Joshua,

the High Priest, and Zerubbabel, the Civil Leader **(Zechariah 4:2-3, 11:14)**, who were raised up as light ready to carry their prophetic witness through power supplied by the Holy Spirit.
- h. The Throng – **vs. 9-10**
    1. The people rejoice that the two witnesses are dead. They make merry and send gifts one to another because the two prophets tormented them. The world hates God's people and especially God's preachers.
- i. The Terror – **vs. 11**
    1. Right in the midst of their rejoicing, God resurrects the two prophets and great fear will fall upon those who see them. God will vindicate His messengers by raising them from the dead. The prophets' resurrection will cause great fear terrorizing the unbelieving world. **(vs. 11)**
- j. The Transition – **vs. 12**
    1. *"...Come up hither..."* – **vs. 12**
        - After the people witness this, do they repent? No!
        - The rich man in hell cried ***"...Father Abraham have mercy upon me..."***. The rich man wanted Lazarus to be sent back from the dead to warn his brothers. Abraham responded, they have Moses and the prophets and if they hear not Moses and the prophets, neither will they be persuaded though one rose from the dead. **(Luke 16:24, 30-31)**
        - Here in Revelation 11, not just one but two were raised from the dead, and still they did not repent. Their enemies, religion, and the whole world watched as these men went to Heaven, but they did not believe.

The Second Woe

IV. THE VISITATION – vs. 13-14

    a. *"[13] And the same hour was there a great earthquake, and the tenth part of the city fell, and in the earthquake were slain of men seven thousand: and the remnant were affrighted, and gave glory to the God of heaven. [14] The second woe is past; and behold, the third woe cometh quickly."* – Revelation 11:13-14

    b. *"And the same hour was there a great earthquake..."* – vs. 13

        1. An earthquake attended both the death and resurrection of Christ. **(Matthew 27:51 and 28:2)**

    c. In verse 13 we have two numbers, 10 and 7. These two are God's perfect numbers. Number 10 means "perfection of Divine order". Number 7 means "complete". This is God's complete destruction.

        1. The Victims – vs. 13
- 7000 men are slain. What a terrible price to pay for the treatment of God's two witnesses.
- *"Saying, Touch not mine anointed, and do my prophets no harm."* – Psalm 105:15

The Third Woe

V. THE VOICES AND THE SEVENTH TRUMPET – vs. 14-15

    a. *"[14] The second woe is past; and behold, the third woe cometh quickly. [15] And the seventh angel sounded; and there were great voices in heaven, saying, The kingdoms of this world are become the kingdoms of our Lord, and of His Christ; and He shall reign for ever and ever."* – Revelation 11:14-15

    b. This is the end of the second parenthetical passage.

    c. The trumpet judgements are resumed.

- d. The blowing of the seventh trumpet introduces the third woe and contains the seven vial judgements, which are not poured out upon the earth until later in **Revelation 16:1-17**.
- e. Following the breaking of the fifth seal in **Revelation 6:9-11**, the martyrs cry *"How long, O Lord, holy and true doest thou not avenge our blood upon them that dwell on the earth?"*
  1. The answer came when the seventh trumpet sounded. A great shout will go up in heaven and the inhabitants see through to the end of **Revelation 20**.
  2. The Victor – **vs. 15**
  3. "Christ"

VI. THE VICTORY – vs. 16-18

- a. *"[16] And the four and twenty elders, which sat before God on their seats, fell upon their faces, and worshipped God, [17] Saying, We give thee thanks, O Lord God Almighty, which art, and wast, and art to come; because Thou hast taken to Thee Thy great power, and hast reigned. [18] And the nations were angry, and Thy wrath is come, and the time of the dead, that they should be judged, and that Thou shouldest give reward unto Thy servants the prophets, and to the saints, and them that fear Thy name, small and great; and shouldest destroy them which destroy the earth."* – **Revelation 11:16-18**
- b. In verse 16, the four and twenty elders fell upon their faces and worshipped God.
- c. In verse 17 they thank God for who He is.
  1. *"...thou hast taken to Thee Thy great power, and hast reigned..."* (vs. 17).
     - This is a reference to Christ's thousand-year reign here on the earth.
  2. *"And the nations were angry..."* (vs. 18)
     - *"Why do the heathen rage, and the people imagine a vain thing?"* – **Psalm 2:1**

- *"The heathen raged, the kingdoms were moved: he uttered his voice, the earth melted." – Psalm 46:6*
- The reason why the nations are angry, they know that this is the time of judgement for unbelievers who are cast into the lake of fire.

3. *"...Thy wrath is come..."* (vs. 18)
   - The bottom line is, the wicked do not get off scot-free. No one gets away with anything. Sooner or later, God will catch up with them and they will get their just desserts. This is the day of retribution.

4. *"...the time of the dead, that they should be judged..."* (vs. 18)
   - This is speaking of the Great White Throne judgement in **Revelation 20:11-15**.

5. *"...Thou shouldest give reward unto Thy servants..."* (vs. 18)
   - The servants and the prophets means Moses and all the prophets.

6. *"...and to the saints..."* (vs. 18)
   - This means the tribulation saints.
   - The Church saints are in heaven and have already been rewarded at the Judgement Seat of Christ. Read the following Scriptures:
     - **Psalm 62:12**
     - **Jeremiah 17:10**
     - **Matthew 16:27**
     - **Romans 2:6**
     - **II Corinthians 5:10**
     - **I Peter 1:17**
     - **I Corinthians 3:11-15**

7. *"...destroy them which destroy the earth."* – (vs. 18)
   - God will destroy every kind of wickedness on the earth before setting up the Millennial Kingdom **(Revelation 19:17-21)**.

VII. THE VISION – vs. 19

a. *"And the temple of God was opened in heaven, and there was seen in His temple the ark of His testament: and there were lightnings, and voices, and thunderings, and an earthquake, and great hail."* – **Revelation 11:19**

b. In the Old Testament, the Ark of the Covenant was a token of God's presence. It comes before us for the first time since the Babylonian captivity. The sins of Israel caused God to withdraw His presence from among them. This implies that they were not living holy lives.

c. Restoration of the Ark means the restoration of God's presence among Israel.

d. There is coming a day when all remembrance of the Ark and worship connected with it shall forever pass away.
   1. **Jeremiah 3:12-17**
   2. **Revelation 21:22**

Revelation – Chapter 12

War in Heaven

The middle of the week of seven years is reached or passed in the killing of the two witnesses in **Revelation 11:7**. The anti-Christ has broken his covenant with Israel. Great tribulation is on in all its fury.

The Woman: Israel

I. **THE WONDER WOMAN – vs. 1-2**
   a. *"[1] And there appeared a great wonder in heaven; a woman clothed with the sun, and the moon under her feet, and upon her head a crown of twelve stars: [2] And she being with child cried, travailing in birth, and pained to be delivered."* – Revelation 12:1-2
   b. The woman, being a sign, is symbolic.
      1. Of whom is she symbolic? The answer is in **Genesis 37:9-10**. Jacob understands the sun, the moon, and the stars to represent his people. Israel is pictured as a woman **(Isaiah 7:14; 54:1-6; 66:7-8)**. The woman is a symbol of Israel from whom Christ came according to the flesh **(Galatians 4:4)**.

Satan

II. **THE WOEFUL DRAGON – vs. 3-4**
   a. *"[3] And there appeared another wonder in heaven; and behold a great red dragon, having seven heads and ten horns, and seven crowns upon his heads. [4] And his tail drew the third part of the stars of heaven, and did cast them to the earth: and the dragon stood before the woman*

which was ready to be delivered, for to devour her child as soon as it was born." – Revelation 12:3

b. His Name – **vs. 3**
   1. The great red dragon is Satan himself **(Revelation 12:9)**.
   2. Red speaks of his murderous bloodthirsty character. He was a murderer from the beginning **(John 8:44)**.
c. His Seven Heads – **vs. 3**
   1. The number seven (7) speaks of completeness. The heads speak of wisdom.
   2. **Ezekiel 28:12-17** describes Satan in his position as an exalted angel before his fall.
      - In Satan's unfallen state, he was the model of perfection, full of wisdom, and perfect beauty **(vs. 12)**.
      - Satan's beauty is described in dazzling display of brilliant stones **(vs. 13)**.
      - At that time, Satan was on the holy mount of God suggesting his position of honor about the throne of God **(vs. 14)**.
      - **Verse 15** further disallows identification with the King of Tyrus. Satan was blameless as a cherub until he sinned. The sin is more fully described in his fall in **Isaiah 14:13-14**. Satan desired preeminence like God.
      - As a result he was cast out of Heaven, away from his place of exaltation **(vs. 16)**.
      - The cause of Satan's sin is identified as pride **(vs. 17)**.
      - Satan today, as a roaring lion walketh about seeking whom he may devour **(I Peter 5:8)**.
d. His Ten Horns – **vs. 3**
   1. The ten (10) horns speak of governmental power. At the close of this age, there shall be a confederation of ten kingdoms **(Revelation 17:12)**.
e. His Seven Crowns – **vs. 3**
   1. This suggests rulership.
f. His Tail – **vs. 4**

              1. His tail drew the third part of the stars. This was probably fallen angels.
- g. His Position – **vs. 4**
    1. He stood before the woman to destroy her child.
    2. This is exactly what Satan did at the birth of Christ **(Matthew 2:16)**.

The Man-Child: Christ

III. THE WONDERFUL CHILD – vs. 5-6
- a. *"[5] And she brought forth a man child, who was to rule all nations with a rod of iron: and her child was caught up unto God, and to his throne. [6] And the woman fled into the wilderness, where she hath a place prepared of God, that they should feed her there a thousand two hundred and threescore days."* – Revelation 12:5-6
- b. This man child is Christ.
- c. His name shall be called wonderful **(Isaiah 9:6)**. The word wonderful means "a miracle".
    1. His birth was a miracle – virgin born – **Isaiah 7:14, Matthew 1:23**
    2. His life was a miracle – *"...knew no sin..."* – **II Corinthians 5:21**
    3. His death was a miracle – *"...I have power to lay it down..."* – **John 10:18**
    4. His resurrection was a miracle – *"...I have power to take it up again..."* – **John 10:18**
    5. His ascension was a miracle – **Act 1:10-11**
        - *"...Child was caught up unto God..."* – **vs. 5**
        - This is a reference to His ascension.
    6. His second coming will be a miracle – **Zechariah 14:1-7**
        - He will be the ruler of all nations – **vs. 5** and **Psalm 2:8-9**.
            ❖ Christ has not ruled all nations yet, but He will.

REVELATION—CHAPTER 12

> ❖ The rod of iron speaks of capital punishment.

d. This is Israel's flight in the tribulation time **(vs. 6)**.
e. The place is in the mountains **(Matthew 24:16)**.
f. **Daniel 11:41** tells us that Edom, Moab, and the children of Ammon will escape the hand of the anti-Christ. No doubt the Jews will find a place of refuge in these countries. Probably the city of Petra, which is already chiseled out of solid rock and empty awaiting the time for Israel to come and occupy. Read **Isaiah 16:1-4**. In verse 1, you will find the word "Sela" meaning Petra.
g. One thousand two hundred and threescore days (1260) is 3½ years. This is the last half of the 70th week in Daniel and is the last half of the great tribulation.

The Archangel

IV. THE WAR IN HEAVEN – vs. 7-12

a. *"[7] And there was war in heaven: Michael and his angels fought against the dragon; and the dragon fought and his angels, [8] And prevailed not; neither was their place found any more in heaven. [9] And the great dragon was cast out, that old serpent, called the Devil, and Satan, which deceiveth the whole world: he was cast out into the earth, and his angels were cast out with him. [10] And I heard a loud voice saying in heaven, Now is come salvation, and strength, and the kingdom of our God, and the power of his Christ: for the accuser of our brethren is cast down, which accused them before our God day and night. [11] And they overcame him by the blood of the Lamb, and by the word of their testimony; and they loved not their lives unto the death. [12] Therefore rejoice, ye heavens, and ye that dwell in them. Woe to the inhabiters of the earth and of the sea! For the devil is come down unto you, having great wrath, because he knoweth that he hath but a short time." –* **Revelation 12:7-12**

    b.   The Conflict – **vs. 7-8**
        1.   ***"...Michael and his angels fought against the dragon; and the dragon fought and his angels..."*** **– (vs. 7)**
        2.   Here we have warfare in heaven. This conflict has always been going on, but now, it breaks out in open war. Michael and his angels win the war.
        3.   The name Michael means "one like unto God". He defends the destiny of God's elect nation, Israel **(Daniel 10:21 and 12:1)**.
        4.   Satan's four defeats and his being cast down:
- The 1st defeat – **Isaiah 14:12-17; Ezekiel 28:12-17** – (past)
- The 2nd defeat – **John 19:30, Matthew 28:1-6** – (past – Calvary)
- The 3rd defeat – **Revelation 12:7-9** – (future – in tribulation time)
- The 4th defeat – **Revelation 20:1-3** – (future)
    - ❖ At the Second Coming of Christ, Satan will be defeated and cast down into the bottomless pit to be chained for a 1000 years.

    c.   The Casting Out – **vs. 9-10**
        1.   Satan has long had access to the throne of God **(Job 1:6-12)**. Why we do not know he is always an accuser of the brethren day and night? Satan never takes a vacation and he never sleeps. He is on the job 24 hours a day. Satan will never again cross the threshold of Heaven.

    d.   The Cleansing – **vs. 11**
        1.   Cleansing comes for the believers in three ways
- By the blood of the Lamb
- By the word of their testimony
- They loved not their lives unto death. Our victory is in the cross of Jesus.

REVELATION—CHAPTER 12

V. THE WRATH OF SATAN – vs. 12-13
    a. *"[12]... For the devil is come down unto you, having great wrath, because he knoweth that he hath but a short time. [13] And when the dragon saw that he was cast unto the earth, he persecuted the woman which brought forth the man child."* – **Revelation 12:12-13**
    b. *"...rejoice, ye heavens, and ye that dwell in them..."* – **vs. 12**
        1. Heaven rejoices because these witnesses on earth were completely committed to Christ.
    c. Satan comes down in great wrath
        1. This means Satan is on the earth in full power.
    d. *"...he knoweth that he hath but a short time..."* – **vs. 12**
        1. This is the last 3½ years of the great tribulation. Satan, now so bent on rule or ruin, he is aroused to great wrath and determined to have his way at any cost.
    e. *"...he persecuted the woman..."* (Israel) – **vs. 13**
    f. *"And to the woman were given two wings of a great eagle, that she might fly into the wilderness, into her place, where she is nourished for a time, and times, and half a time, from the face of the serpent."* – **Revelation 12:14**
        1. Go back and read comments made on **Revelation 12:6**.

VI. THE WATER OF SATAN – vs. 15-16
    a. *"[15] And the serpent cast out of his mouth water as a flood after the woman, that he might cause her to be carried away of the flood. [16] And the earth helped the woman, and the earth opened her mouth, and swallowed up the flood which the dragon cast out of his mouth."* – **Revelation 12:15-16**
    b. Satan can cause miracles. He will attack with a flood in order to drown God's people out of their wilderness refuge.
    c. God in turn will cause the earth to open and consume the flood and save His people.

1. Satan gives water of death
2. Christ gives water of life

The Jewish Remnant

VII. THE WAR OF SATAN – vs. 17

a. *"And the dragon was wroth with the woman, and went to make war with the remnant of her seed, which keep the commandments of God, and have the testimony of Jesus Christ."* – **Revelation 12:17**
b. The failure of Satan in verses 15 and 16 rouses his wrath and rage. He goes to make war with the remnant of her seed.
c. If we keep God's commandments, we will also face the rage of Satan.

Revelation – Chapter 13

The Beast Out of the Sea & The Beast Out of the Earth

In Chapter 13 we have the Dragon, the Beast out of the Sea and the Beast out of the Earth. This is the satanic trinity.

- The Dragon – the Devil – He is the one who imitates God the Father.
- The Beast out of the Sea – the anti-Christ – He is the one who imitates our Lord Jesus Christ.
- The Beast out of the Earth – the False Prophet – He is the one who imitates the Holy Spirit. **(Revelation 16:13)**

The First Beast – The anti-Christ

I. **THE DESCRIPTION – vs. 1**
    a.   *"[1] And I stood upon the sand of the sea, and saw a beast rise up out of the sea, having seven heads and ten horns, and upon his horns ten crowns, and upon his heads the name of blasphemy. [2] And the beast which I saw was like unto a leopard, and his feet were as the feet of a bear, and his mouth as the mouth of a lion: and the dragon gave him his power, and his seat, and great authority."* – Revelation 13:1-2

    b.   The First Beast
        1.   The anti-Christ is a political power and person.
        2.   He rises up out of the sea. The sea represents the restless nations.
- *"But the wicked are like the troubled sea, when it cannot rest, whose waters cast up mire and dirt."* – Isaiah 57:20
- In **Revelation 17:15**, the waters are:
  - People
  - Multitudes
  - Nations

3. Coming events are casting their foreshadows, and Bible prophecy and world history is moving toward a climax. Nations today are restless, raging, and rebelling against God. **(Psalm 2:1-3)**
  - ❖ Tongues

c. The Seven Heads
  1. This is not easily identified.
     - The first view is that some believe the heads were certain Roman Emperors.
     - The second view is that others believe the heads represent seven forms of government through which Rome passed.
     - The third view is that the heads represent seven great nations of the ancient times, which blasphemed God.
       - ❖ Roman Empire
       - ❖ Greece
       - ❖ Media-Persia
       - ❖ Persia
       - ❖ Babylon
       - ❖ Egypt
       - ❖ Assyria
  2. The Kingdom of the Beast would be the seventh, which is yet to come. All these blasphemed God. The seven heads are interpreted as seven kings in **Revelation 17:9-10**. I believe the third view is the correct one.

d. *"...the ten horns, and upon his horns ten crowns..."* – vs. 13
  1. The 10 horns are 10 kings or kingdoms **(Revelation 17:12)**.
  2. The Beast is the leader of a 10 Federation Kingdom that shall rise out of Western Europe.

e. *"...upon his heads the name of blasphemy..."* – vs. 13
  1. The kingdom of the anti-Christ will be one of blasphemy against God.
  2. Blasphemy means:
     - Speaking Evil
     - Slanderous
     - Railing

- f. Like unto a lion, a bear, and a leopard – **vs. 2**
  1. In Daniel Chapter 7, in the vision, the first beast Daniel saw was like a lion.
     - The lion represents Babylon.
  2. The second beast Daniel saw was like a bear.
     - The bear represents Media-Persia.
  3. The third beast Daniel saw was like a leopard.
     - The leopard represents Greece.
  4. The anti-Christ will combine all the characteristics of whatever the Babylonian, Media-Persian, and Grecian Empires had of strength, brutality, and swiftness. He receives his power from the dragon (the devil). He is sold out to the devil.

II. THE DEADLY WOUND – vs. 3

a. *"And I saw one of his heads as it were wounded to death; and his deadly wound was healed: and all the world wondered after the beast."* – Revelation 13:3

b. The anti-Christ is actually killed and Satan restores him to life.
   - *"...wounded to death..."* literally reads "as having been slain to death". This is the same word (slain) that was used in Revelation 5:6 when it speaks of the Lamb "as it had been slain".
   - Since Christ actually died, it would appear that this ruler will actually die. His wound healed which can only mean life restored.
   - The anti-Christ duplicates Christ's resurrection.
   - It should be mentioned that Satan has no power but what God's allows him.

c. The Delusion – **vs. 3**
   - *"...all the world wondered after the beast."* – **vs. 3**
   - *"[10] And with all deceivableness of unrighteousness in them that perish; because they received not the love of the truth, that they might be saved. [11] And for this cause God*

shall send them strong delusion, that they should believe a lie:" – II Thessalonians 2:10-11
- They rejected the one true Christ and believed the big lie that the anti-Christ is God.
  - ❖ *"I am come in My Father's Name, and ye receive Me not: if another shall come in his own name, him ye will receive." – John 5:43*

VIII. THE DRAGON – vs. 4
a. *"And they worshipped the dragon which gave power unto the beast: and they worshipped the beast, saying, Who is like unto the beast? Who is able to make war with him?" – Revelation 13:4*
b. The world is headed for complete devil worship.
- In verse 3 we had the world's admiration of the beast (the anti-Christ).
- In verse 4 we have the world worshipping the dragon (the devil).
  - ❖ This is what the devil has always wanted. He wants to be worshipped.
  - ❖ He will make the world believe that evil is good, that dark is day, that light is dark, that black is white, that up is down, etc.

IX. THE DECEPTION – vs. 5
a. *"And there was given unto him a mouth speaking great things and blasphemies; and power was given unto him to continue forty and two months." – Revelation 13:5*
b. *"[9] Even him, whose coming is after the working of Satan with all power and signs and lying wonders, [10] And with all deceivableness of unrighteousness in them that perish; because they received not the love of the truth, that they might be saved." – II Thessalonians 2:9-10*
c. *"...there was given unto him a mouth..." – vs. 5*
  1. He has a capacity to speak, to bellow forth, spew forth blasphemies against God.

REVELATION—CHAPTER 13

- *"And he shall speak great words against the most High, and shall wear out the saints of the most High, and think to change times and laws: and they shall be given into his hand until a time and times and the dividing of time."* – Daniel 7:25
  - ❖ Time means 1 year
  - ❖ Times means 2 years
  - ❖ Dividing of time means ½ year
- This is the reign of anti-Christ. It will be the last 3½ years of the tribulation period.

d. *"...power was given unto him to continue forty and two months..."* – vs. 5
  1. This begins in the middle of the seven-year tribulation and will last 3½ years.
  2. This power is power over the world to sway them. It was given by the Divine permissive will of God.

X. THE DEFIANCE – vs. 6

a. *"And he opened his mouth in blasphemy against God, to blaspheme His Name, and His tabernacle, and them that dwell in heaven."* – Revelation 13:6

b. *"...opened his mouth in blasphemy..."* – vs. 6
  1. He pours forth profanity, blasphemies, and derision against heaven and the Holy God.

c. *"...against God, to blaspheme His Name..."* – vs. 6
  1. It will be directed toward God to blaspheme His Name continually and to incite others to blaspheme. **(Revelation 16:9, 11, 21)**

d. *"...and His tabernacle..."* – vs. 6
  1. This is God's dwelling place. It is a worship place belonging to Him and known as His.

e. *"...and them that dwell in heaven..."* – vs. 6
  1. He will blaspheme those that dwell in heaven.
  2. The Lord will allow this to continue for 3½ years until the great tribulation is over and our Lord comes to rule.

XI. **THE DESTRUCTION** – vs. 7

    a. *"And it was given unto him to make war with the saints, and to over come them: and power was given him over all kindreds, and tongues, and nations."* – **Revelation 13:7**

    b. The first beast (the anti-Christ) shows that he hates God by attacking His people on earth. At first he will succeed **(Daniel 7:21)** and gain control over all men of every nation.

    c. But God is still on the throne. **(Revelation 19:11)**

    d. All the torture and terror experienced in the last 60 centuries will be at his command. This is the last war on God's people. His power is limited to 42 months.

XII. **THE DARKNESS** – vs. 8

    a. *"And all that dwell upon the earth shall worship him, whose names are not written in the book of life of the Lamb slain from the foundation of the world."* – **Revelation 13:8**

    b. Spiritual darkness shall cover the earth and gross darkness shall cover the people **(Isaiah 60:1-2)**.
        1. This is the darkest hour in the history of the world.

    c. The beast is a world dictator. The whole world worships him with the exception of those whose names are written in the Lamb's book of life.

XIII. **THE DELIVERANCE** – vs. 9

    a. *"If any man have an ear, let him hear."* – **Revelation 13:9**

    b. Hear what? God's Word and the Holy Spirit. The Word of God will comfort and strengthen God's people during the tribulation, even as it does today. So, we should listen to what the Holy Spirit says. **(Revelation 2:11)**

XI. THE DANGER – vs. 10
    a. ***"He that leadeth into captivity shall go into captivity: he that killeth with the sword must be killed with the sword. Here is the patience and the faith of the saints." – Revelation 13:10***
    b. The warning is not to resist the beast. This is his day. God is permitting him to go to the limit. Many saints will be killed, but there is no use to resist him.
    c. Here he adds also that God will punish those who kill others or make them prisoners. The same thing will happen to them. **(Exodus 21:12)**
        1. All men will be judged according to their works. **(Revelation 20:12)**

The Second Beast – The False Prophet

The Second Beast is the False Prophet, a religious power and a person.

I. THE PLACE HE CAME FROM – vs. 11
    a. ***"And I beheld another beast coming up out of the earth; and he had two horns like a lamb, and he spake as a dragon." – Revelation 13:11***
    b. **"…beast coming up out of the earth…" – vs. 11**
        1. This wild beast comes up out of the masses of people of the earth.
    c. Many natural men love power, others love religion. It is clear that man's heart runs after either intellect or power. If his conscience is still active his heart runs into religion to quiet it.
    d. The devil could not accomplish his plan if there were no earthly religions.
    e. Satan will put forth two main leaders of systems that express human nature on either side, which will exactly suit what man's heart seeks after.
    f. The second beast has two horns like a lamb.
        1. He wants to appear as the Lamb of God (Jesus).
        2. However, his words show that he is from Satan.

- *"...he spake as a dragon..."* – vs. 11

II. **THE POWER HE EXERCISES** – vs. 12
    a. ***"And he exerciseth all the power of the first beast before him, and causeth the earth and them which dwell therein to worship the first beast, whose deadly wound was healed."*** – **Revelation 13:12**
    b. The Second Beast (the False Prophet) exercises the power of the First Beast (the anti-Christ) to cause everyone to worship the First Beast (the anti-Christ).
        1. The two of them work hand in hand. They are in it together. Both of them are marching to the beat of the same drum.
        2. We can look at it like this:
- He is the organizer and propagator of a new religion, which is focused on the anti-Christ.
- The mindset is that which says he deserves to be worshipped and acclaimed because he is one who has come back from the dead.
  ❖ He exalts the anti-Christ.
  ❖ He promotes religion.

III. **THE PLAN** – vs. 13-17
    a. ***"[13] And he doeth great wonders, so that he maketh fire come down from heaven on the earth in the sight of men, [14] And deceiveth them that dwell on the earth by the means of those miracles which he had power to do in the sight of the beast; saying to them that dwell on the earth, that they should make an image to the beast, which had the wound by a sword, and did live. [15] And he had power to give life unto the image of the beast, that the image of the beast should both speak, and cause that as many as would not worship the image of the beast should be killed. [16] And he causeth all, both small and great, rich and poor, free and bond, to receive a mark in their right***

REVELATION—CHAPTER 13

hand, or in their foreheads: [17] And that no man might buy or sell, save he that had the mark, or the name of the beast, or the number of his name." – **Revelation 13:13-17**

    b.   He does great wonders – **vs. 13**
          1.   He's a miracle worker
    c.   He calls fire down from heaven – **vs. 13**
    d.   He uses deception – **vs. 14**
    e.   He gives life to the image – **vs. 15**
    f.   He makes the image speak – **vs. 15**
    g.   He kills those who would not worship the beast – **vs. 15**
    h.   He causes all, both small and great, rich and poor to receive the mark of the beast – **vs. 16-17**
- The Second Beast carries out the mandate that no one can buy or sell legally without the mark of the name or number of the First Beast.
- John has revealed a prevalent satanic system that will control the world during the great tribulation. Discerning believers are acutely aware that the seeds of this movement are being sown today and could blossom in the very near future.

Just remember that the saved of our age (the Church age) will be in heaven with Christ during the tribulation period.

If you are not a Christian, let me encourage you to be saved today. Don't take a chance on living until tomorrow. Christ may come at any moment. Tomorrow may begin the awful day of the great tribulation.

IV.   THE PRESUMPTUOUS MAN – vs. 18

    a.   *"Here is wisdom. Let him that hath understanding count the number of the beast: for it is the number of a man; and his number is Six hundred three score and six."* – **Revelation 13:18**
    b.   This is the anti-Christ. He will be bold, daring and proud.
    c.   Daniel spent a night in the lion's den and came out the next morning unshaken. He faced kings unafraid. But when he saw the beast, he fainted.

1. *"And I Daniel fainted, and was sick certain days; afterward I rose up, and did the king's business; and I was astonished at the vision, but none understood it."* – Daniel 8:27

d. Who is this person?
   1. Some have said that the Pope is the anti-Christ. Others have said Napoleon, Hitler, Stalin, Mussolini, and others were possibly the anti-Christ. But none of these were. He is Satan's special agent, the second person of the evil trinity. The other two parts of the evil trinity are Satan himself who counterfeit God the Father and the False Prophet who counterfeits God the Holy Spirit. The anti-Christ is the counterfeit of the Lord Jesus Christ and he will not be revealed until after the rapture of the Church **(II Thessalonians 2:3)**.

d. The names of the anti-Christ are:
   1. The wicked one – **Psalm 10:2, 4**
   2. The little horn – **Daniel 7:8**
   3. King of fierce countenance – **Daniel 8:23**
   4. The prince that shall come – **Daniel 9:26**
   5. The vile person – **Daniel 11:21**
   6. The willful king – **Daniel 11:36**
   7. The idol shepherd – **Zechariah 11:16-17**
   8. The abomination of desolation – **Matthew 24:15**
   9. The anti-Christ – **I John 2:22**
   10. The man of sin – **II Thessalonians 2:3**
   11. The lawless one – **II Thessalonians 2:8**
   12. The beast out of the sea – **Revelation 11:7, 13:1-10**

Revelation – Chapter 14

Vision of the Lamb and the 144,000

Revelation 14 looks back to the beginning of the tribulation and forward to the end of the tribulation and on into the millennium.

I. **THE LOOK** – vs. 1
    a. *"And I looked, and lo, a Lamb stood on the mount Sion, and with Him an hundred forty and four thousand, having His Father's name written in their foreheads."* – Revelation 14:1
    b. *"And I looked..."* – vs. 1
        1. The word "looked" means to gaze with wide-open eyes at something remarkable.
    c. The Lamb – **vs. 1**
        1. John clearly saw the Lamb.
            • *"The next day John seeth Jesus coming unto him and saith, Behold the Lamb of God, which taketh away the sin of the world."* – John 1:29
        2. The word Lamb is used 27 times in Revelation.
    d. The Location – **vs. 1**
        1. Mount Sion
            • This is a mountain in Jerusalem.
            • From the time of David, this was the seat of government for Israel.
            • Sion is mentioned 156 times in the Bible. Jerusalem is mentioned 828 times. These two terms are sometimes used interchangeably. Sion represents the whole city of Jerusalem.
            • One day Jesus will reign from Jerusalem in Mount Sion. **(Psalm 2:6, Isaiah 24:23)**

II. **THE LIVING SAINTS** – vs. 1-2

    a. *"[1] And I looked, and lo, a Lamb stood on the mount Sion, and with Him an hundred forty and four thousand, having His Father's name written in their foreheads. [2] And I heard a voice from heaven as the voice of many waters and as the voice of a great thunder: and I heard the voice of harpers harping with their harps:"* – Revelation 14:1-2

    b. Who are the 144,000? Undoubtedly they are those of Chapter 7. They are God's witnesses during the reign of the beast. They will preach the Gospel of the Kingdom. Through their preaching a great multitude, which no man can number, will be saved. **(Revelation 7:9-10)**

    c. The anti-Christ will put into motion every conceivable means of silencing their testimony. But God takes care of His own. **(John 10:27-29)**

III. THE LOVELY SONG – vs. 3

    a. *"And they sung as it were a new song before the throne, and before the four beasts, and the elders: and no man could learn that song but the hundred and forty and four thousand which were redeemed from the earth."* – Revelation 14:3

    b. The song is uniquely that of the 144,000 redeemed from the earth. No one else could learn it.

    c. This is the song of redemption and deliverance.

IV. THE LIKE MINDED – vs. 4-5

    a. *"[4] These are they which were not defiled with women; for they are virgins. These are they which follow the Lamb whithersoever He goeth. These were redeemed from among men, being the firstfruits unto God and to the Lamb. [5] And in their mouth was found no guile: for they are without fault before the throne of God."* – Revelation 14:4-5

    b. *"...These are they which follow the Lamb whithersoever He goeth..."* – vs. 4

    1. *"Let this mind be in you, which was also in Christ Jesus:"* – Philippians 2:5
  c. The 144,000 are called virgins in the sense that they kept their hearts and bodies from fornication, the crowning sin of that day. **(Revelation 9:21, 14:8, 17:2)**
    1. The sin of fornication is rapidly increasing and growing in our day. Coming events are casting their foreshadows.
  d. *"...being the firstfruits unto God and to the Lamb."* – vs. 4
    1. Firstfruits always indicate more to follow.
    2. A great host of Israelites will be saved in the last half (3½ years) of the tribulation, especially at the end. **(Matthew 24:31, Romans 11:25-27)**
    3. They have been kept from the false religion of the tribulation. Their lives have not been stained with the terrible sins of the day.

V. THE LIVING EVERLASTING GOSPEL – vs. 6-7

  a. *"[6] And I saw another angel fly in the midst of heaven, having the everlasting Gospel to preach unto them that dwell on the earth, and to every nation, and kindred, and tongue, and people, [7] Saying with a loud voice, Fear God, and give glory to Him: for the hour of His judgment is come: and worship Him that made heaven, and earth, and the sea, and the fountains of waters."* – Revelation 14:6-7
  b. Verse 6 takes us back into the tribulation. Here the angel is preaching the everlasting Gospel warning men against the worship of the beast. The message of the angel is called the everlasting Gospel. Only one Gospel has been preached through the ages, but, it has various phases. It is the Gospel of the Kingdom **(Matthew 24:14)**. Whether it be the Gospel of the Kingdom or the Gospel of the Grace of God, it is the same and eternal. In the tribulation, the Gospel will have the Kingdom emphasis.

    c.   *"...Fear God..." – vs. 7*
        1.   *"Serve the Lord with fear, and rejoice with trembling." – Psalm 2:11*
    d.   *"...give glory to Him..." – vs. 7*
        1.   The word "glory" means to be clear, to shine, to give light, to praise.
    e.   *"...the hour of His judgment is come..." – vs. 7*
        1.   The Gospel has always had an element of Judgment.
- *"He that believeth and is baptized shall be saved; but he that believeth not shall be damned." – Mark 16:16*
- *"For by one Spirit are we all baptized into one body, whether we be Jews or Gentiles, whether we be bond or free; and have been all made to drink into one Spirit." – I Corinthians 12:13*

    f.   *"...worship Him..." – vs. 7*
        1.   The word "worship" means to kiss. Such as a dog licking his master's hand.
        2.   The kiss was a sign of reconciliation, affection, and allegiance even though Judas abused it. It need not be abandoned. Don't be ashamed to embrace the Lord and give Him honor and glory.
- *"Kiss the Son, lest he be angry and ye perish from the way, when His wrath is kindled but a little. Blessed are all they that put their trust in Him." – Psalm 2:12*

VI.   THE LASCIVIOUS CITY – vs. 8
    a.   *"And there followed another angel, saying, Babylon is fallen, is fallen, that great city, because she made all nations drink of the wine of the wrath of her fornication." – Revelation 14:8*
    b.   This verse points to chapters 17 and 18 when political and ecclesiastical Babylon will be destroyed. Her judgment is so sure that it appears to have already happened.

REVELATION—CHAPTER 14

VII. THE LOSS OF SOUL – vs. 9-12
    a. *"[9] And the third angel followed them, saying with a loud voice, If any man worship the beast and his image, and receive his mark in his forehead, or in his hand, [10] The same shall drink of the wine of the wrath of God, which is poured out without mixture into the cup of his indignation; and he shall be tormented with fire and brimstone in the presence of the holy angels and in the presence of the Lamb: [11] And the smoke of their torment ascendeth up for ever and ever; and they have no rest day nor night, who worship the beast and his image, and whosoever receiveth the mark of his name. [12] Here is the patience of the saints: here are they that keep the commandments of God, and the faith of Jesus."* – **Revelation 14:9-12**
    b. The Warning of the Angel – **vs. 9**
    c. The Wrath of God – **vs. 10-11**
    d. The Waiting Saints – **vs. 12**
        1. They keep the commandments of God. It will take great patience and endurance to be true to God in that day when the beast rules.
        2. The trials we suffer now are only child's play. We talk of persecution today, we should be ashamed to use the word!
    e. Those who worship the beast and his image will be lost forever.
    f. You may lose your money, your job, your land, your health, your family, but your soul loss is the most tragic loss.
        1. *"For what shall it profit a man , if he shall gain the whole world, and lose his own soul?"* – **Mark 8:36**

VIII. THE LABOURERS – vs. 13
    a. *"And I heard a voice from heaven saying unto me, Write, Blessed are the dead which die in the Lord from henceforth: Yea, saith the Spirit, that they may rest from their labours; and their works do follow them."* – **Revelation 14:13**

    b. The anti-Christ may be permitted to put the saints to death, but God says they are blessed.
    c. It will be better to be dead than to be alive in that day. They are at rest, their works follow them, and their reward is certain. **(Revelation 22:12)**

The Vision of Armageddon

I. <u>**THE CLOUD**</u> **– vs. 14**
   a. *"And I looked, and behold a white cloud, and upon the cloud one sat like unto the Son of man, having on His head a golden crown, and in His hand a sharp sickle."* – Revelation 14:14
   b. The Cloud speaks of :
       1. God's presence – **Exodus 14:19-21**
       2. He ascended back to heaven in a cloud – **Acts 1:9**
       3. He is coming the second time with clouds – **Matthew 24:30**
       4. The clouds are His chariot – **Psalm 104:3**
   c. The Christ of God – **vs. 14**
       1. God the Father has committed all judgment to Jesus Christ, the Son. So, He now exercises judgment with authority.
           - *"For the Father judgeth no man, but hath committed all judgement unto the Son:"* – John 5:22
   d. The Crown of Gold – **vs. 14**
       1. The golden crown speaks of Christ's kingship.
       2. The sharp sickle speaks of Christ's Second Coming to execute judgment. **(Revelation 19)**

II. <u>**THE CRYING**</u> **– vs. 15**
   a. *"And another angel came out of the temple, crying with a loud voice to him that sat on the cloud, Thrust in thy sickle, and reap: for the time is come*

REVELATION—CHAPTER 14

          for thee to reap; for the harvest of the earth is ripe." – Revelation 14:15
- b. This is the cry for reaping.
  1. This earth will reap what she has sown for the last 6,000 years.
  2. Man has sown sin and rebellion against God. Now man must reap the judgment of God.
  3. The word "ripe" means rotten. This world is not getting better. At the reaping time, it will be rotten with sin.
- c. The other two angels in verses 17 and 18 are Christ's helpers in this reaping.

III. THE CLUSTERS AND THE CASTING – vs. 18-19

- a. *"[18] And another angel came out from the altar, which had power over fire; and cried with a loud cry to him that had the sharp sickle, saying, Thrust in thy sharp sickle, and gather the clusters of the vine of the earth; for her grapes are fully ripe. [19] And the angel thrust in his sickle into the earth, and gathered the vine of the earth, and cast it into the great winepress of the wrath of God." – Revelation 14:18-19*
- b. The vine of the earth is the false religion of the anti-Christ.
- c. Christ is the true vine.
  1. *"I am the vine..." – John 15:5*
- d. Here are all the false religions of man and they are fully ripe and ready for harvest. This was brought about because man refused the life of God and fully developed an apostate religion.
  1. Moses spoke of this day long ago. **(Deuteronomy 32:31-35)**

IV. THE CITY – vs. 20

- a. *"And the winepress was trodden without the city, and blood came out of the winepress, even unto*

        the horse bridles, by the space of a thousand and six hundred furlongs." – Revelation 14:20
- b. Jesus was crucified outside Jerusalem
    1. ***"Wherefore Jesus also, that He might sanctify the people with His own blood, suffered without the gate." – Hebrews 13:12***
- c. So, outside the city in the valley of Jehoshaphat, the valley of judgment, God will complete the trampling down of the wicked.
- d. Blood will run to the horse bridle, approximately 200 miles.
- e. Millions will be killed. It does not bear thinking about.

Revelation – Chapter 15

The Seven Last Vials of God's Wrath

Chapter 15 presents a vision in heaven. Chapter 16 states what happens on earth at the same time. There is rejoicing in heaven, but there is much suffering upon the earth.

I. **THE SIGN** – vs. 1
    a. *"And I saw another sign in heaven, great and marvellous, seven angels having the seven last plagues; for in them is filled up the wrath of God."* – Revelation 15:1
    b. Seven angels carry out the execution of the seven last plagues.
    c. *"...filled up..."* – vs. 1
        1. This means finished, wrath, or literally anger.
    d. These plagues are marked as last because in them the wrath of God is fully spent upon ungodly mankind.

II. **THE SEA** – vs. 2
    a. *"And I saw as it were a sea of glass mingled with fire: and them that had gotten the victory over the beast, and over his image, and over his mark, and over the number of his name, stand on the sea of glass, having the harps of God."* – Revelation 15:2
    b. The sea here and in Chapter 4 suggests the sea of water in the temple, which was used for priestly cleansing.
    c. The sea of crystal is the figure of stability.
    d. The company here and in **Revelation 4:4**, the 24 elders, represents the redeemed of all the ages.
        1. The company here are the tribulation saints.
        2. Both companies no longer need cleansing. They are fixed in their eternal relationship with God.
    e. *"...mingled with fire..."* – vs. 2

1. This speaks of the trials and the tribulations they have come through.

III. THE SONG – vs. 3
    a. ***"And they sing the song of Moses the servant of God, and the song of the Lamb, saying, Great and marvellous are Thy works, Lord God Almighty; just and true are Thy ways, Thou King of saints." – Revelation 15:3***
    b. The song is of deliverance and redemption.
        1. Moses' song was a song of deliverance of Israel from Pharaoh. **(Exodus 15)**
        2. The song of the Lamb is a song of redemption.
        3. Both songs ascribe to God's mighty acts.

IV. THE SACRED WORSHIP – vs. 4
    a. ***"Who shall not fear Thee, O Lord, and glorify Thy Name? for Thou only art holy: for all nations shall come and worship before Thee; for Thy judgments are made manifest." – Revelation 15:4***
    b. Many are deceived about the nature of Jesus.
    c. In heaven, they are not confused about His identity.
        1. *"...the Lamb..."* – vs. 3
        2. *"...Great and marvellous are Thy works..."* – vs. 3
        3. *"...Lord God Almighty..."* – vs. 3
        4. *"...just and true are Thy ways..."* – vs. 3
        5. *"...Thou King of saints..."* – vs. 3
        6. *"...O Lord..."* – vs. 4
        7. *"...for Thou only art holy..."* – vs. 4
        8. *"...Thy judgments are made manifest..."* – vs. 4
    d. The day will come when all people will acknowledge God's wrath, which is about to be poured out. It is deserved righteousness and is perfectly designed to achieve His Holy purpose.

V. THE STRUCTURE – vs. 5

a. *"And after that I looked, and, behold, the temple of the tabernacle of the testimony in heaven was opened:"* – **Revelation 15:5**

b. *"...the temple of the tabernacle of the testimony..."* – **vs. 5**
   1. This was the innermost part of the Holy of Holies. It is the deepest dwelling place of God.
   2. In the Old Testament, the ark contained the two stones of the Law, which were called the Testimony and also called the Ark of the Covenant.
      - *"But they presumed to go up unto the hill top: nevertheless the ark of the covenant of the Lord and Moses, departed not out of the camp."* – **Numbers 14:44**

c. God has always kept His covenant with Israel or anyone who He has entered into a covenant relationship, including the Church.
   1. The New Covenant
      - **Hebrews 8 and 9**

d. The tabernacle in the wilderness, and later the temple in Jerusalem were both a figure of the one in heaven.

e. The true tabernacle is in heaven.
   1. *"[8] Now of the things which we have spoken this is the sum: We have such an high priest, who is set on the right hand of the throne of the Majesty in the heavens; [2] A minister of the sanctuary, and of the true tabernacle, which the Lord pitched, and not man."* – **Hebrews 8:1-2**

VI. THE SEVEN ANGELS – vs. 6-7

a. *"[6] And the seven angels came out of the temple, having the seven plagues, clothed in pure and white linen, and having their breasts girded with golden girdles. [7] And one of the four beasts gave unto the seven angels seven golden vials full of the wrath of God, who liveth for ever and ever."* – **Revelation 15:6-7**

- b. They are priest angels; executioners of God's wrath upon the earth.
- c. They are clothed with garments of a priest.
    1. **"...clothed in pure and white linen, and having their breasts girded with golden girdles..."** – vs. 6
- d. They forsake the work of mercy for the work of judgment.
- e. This is judgment without mercy.
    1. **"...vials full of the wrath of God..."** – vs. 7

VII. <u>**THE SMOKE**</u> – vs. 8
- a. **"And the temple was filled with smoke from the glory of God, and from His power; and no man was able to enter into the temple, till the seven plagues of the seven angels were fulfilled."** – Revelation 15:8
- b. The temple here is seen filled with smoke. When Moses finished the tabernacle and when Solomon had finished the temple, there was a cloud, the "Shekinah Glory", but no smoke.
- c. Smoke means judgment.
    1. The temple is seen full of smoke to reveal the glory and power of God and for judgment.
    2. It is the judgment of the seven vials. **(Revelation 16)**
    3. Smoke is found in connection with judgment 10 times in Revelation.
        - **Revelation 8:4**
        - **Revelation 9:2**
        - **Revelation 9:3**
        - **Revelation 9:17**
        - **Revelation 9:18**
        - **Revelation 14:11**
        - **Revelation 15:8**
        - **Revelation 18:9**
        - **Revelation 18:18**
        - **Revelation 19:3**
- d. The vial judgments are seen as coming from the glory and the power of God.

REVELATION—CHAPTER 15

1. ***"...no man was able to enter into the temple, till the seven plagues of the seven angels were fulfilled..." – vs. 8***
2. This indicates, symbolically, that God will not permit any intercession in the period of the vial judgments.

Revelation – Chapter 16

> The Great Chapter of the Bible
> The Vials of the Wrath of God upon the Earth

I. **<u>THE GREAT VOICE</u> – vs. 1**
    a.   *"And I heard a great voice out of the temple saying to the seven angels, Go your ways, and pour out the vials of the wrath of God upon the earth." –* **Revelation 16:1**
        1.   The word "great" is used eleven (11) times in this chapter.
- **Revelation 16:1**
- **Revelation 16:9**
- **Revelation 16:12**
- **Revelation 16:14**
- **Revelation 16:17**
- **Revelation 16:18** – (two times)
- **Revelation 16:19** – (two times)
- **Revelation 16:21** – (two times)

    b.   This is *"the great and terrible God"* **(Nehemiah 1:5)**, pouring out the vials of wrath upon wicked men on the earth.
    c.   The cup of human iniquity is full. So is the cup of God's wrath.

> The Vials of Wrath

I. **<u>THE GREVIOUS SORE</u> – vs. 2**
    a.   *"And the first went, and poured out his vial upon the earth; and there fell a noisome and grievous sore upon the men which had the mark of the beast, and upon them worshipped his image." –* **Revelation 16:2**
    b.   The First (1st) Vial

REVELATION—CHAPTER 16

      1. They have committed the unforgivable sin.
      2. They have an incurable disease.
      3. The word "noisome" means
- Depraved
- Bad in nature
- Evil
- Wicked

      4. The word "sore" means ulcers.
- They will be running bloody ulcers upon men who worship the beast.
- They will give off a terrible offensive odors.

II. THE GRIP OF DEATH – vs. 3
  a. *"And the second angel poured out his vial upon the sea; and it became as the blood of a dead man: and every living soul died in the sea."* – **Revelation 16:3**
  b. The Second (2nd) Vial
      1. When the second seal was broken, there was bloodshed. – **Revelation 6:3**
      2. In the judgment of the second trumpet, a third part of the life in the sea died. – **Revelation 8:9**
      3. When the second vial of wrath is poured out, all life in the sea dies. – **Revelation 16:3**
      4. The sea is a reservoir of life because of it's salt. When the angel empties his vial of wrath, it becomes a sea of death. All commerce will stop. The stench and disease will be unimaginable.

III. THE GHASTLY SEEN – vs. 4-7
  a. *"[4] And the third angel poured out his vial upon the rivers and fountains of waters; and they became blood. [5] And I heard the angel of the waters say, Thou art righteous, O Lord, which art, and wast, and shalt be, because Thou hast judged thus. [6] For they have shed the blood of saints and prophets, and Thou hast given them blood to*

drink; for they are worthy. [7] And I heard another out of the altar say, Even so, Lord God Almighty, true and righteous are Thy judgments."* – Revelation 16:4-7

    b.   The Third (3rd) Vial
- 1. *"...the rivers and fountains of waters; and they became blood..."* – vs. 4
- 2. The justice of God's judgment.
  - *"...Thou art righteous, O Lord, which art, and wast, and shalt be, because Thou hast judged thus..."* – vs. 5
- 3. The reason the waters were turned to blood.
  - *"For they have shed the blood of saints and prophets..."* – vs. 6
- 4. The retribution of God is poured out upon the wicked for their wicked ways.
  - *"...true and righteous are Thy judgments."* – vs. 7
- 5. Man reaps what he sows.
  - *"Be not deceived; God is not mocked: for whatsoever a man soweth, that shall he also reap."* – Galatians 6:7
  - *"For they have sown the wind, and they shall reap the whirlwind..."* – Hosea 8:7

IV. THE GREAT HEAT – vs. 8-9

    a.   *"[8] And the fourth angel poured out his vial upon the sun; and power was given unto him to scorch men with fire. [9] And men were scorched with great heat, and blasphemed the Name of God, which hath power over these plagues: and they repented not to give Him glory."* – Revelation 16:8-9

    b.   The Fourth (4th) Vial
- 1. During the great tribulation there will be *"signs in the sun, and in the moon, and in the stars; and upon the earth distress of nations, with perplexity; the sea and the waves roaring;"* – Luke 21:25
- 2. The heat of the sun is increased until it scorches men but the response of men shows

how hardened they are in sin. Though they suffer excruciating pain, and know the course of it, they blaspheme God and refuse to repent and give God the glory.
3. Three times in this awesome chapter, verse 9, 11, and 21, it is declared that men reacted to their punishment with blasphemy against God and not with repentance.
4. These judgments are not remedial or corrective in effect, but reveal, all the more, the corruption of those undergoing them.
5. The judgments are punitive. The dwellers on earth are incorrigible (cannot be corrected). Men who will not be drawn by God's love will not be attracted by His wrath.

V. THE GLOOMINESS – vs. 10-11

a. *"[10] And the fifth angel poured out his vial upon the seat of the beast; and his kingdom was full of darkness; and they gnawed their tongues for pain, [11] And blasphemed the God of heaven because of their pains and their sores, and repented not of their deeds."* – Revelation 16:10-11

b. The Fifth (5th) Vial
1. Here men get their fill of darkness.
- *"For, behold, the darkness shall cover the earth, and gross darkness the people;..."* – Isaiah 60:2
- *"A day of darkness and of gloominess, a day of clouds and of thick darkness..."* – Joel 2:2
- This is a preview of the outer darkness of Hell that the unbelievers will suffer.
  ❖ *"And cast ye the unprofitable servant into outer darkness; there shall be weeping and gnashing of teeth."* – Matthew 25:30
- They continued to blaspheme the God of heaven because of their pains and sores, and they repented not of their deeds. They are abandoned to judgment.

EPISODES OF THE END, THE REVELATION OF JESUS CHRIST

VI. THE DRYING UP – vs. 12

   a. *"And the sixth angel poured out his vial upon the great river Euphrates; and the water thereof was dried up, that the way of the kings of the east might be prepared."* – Revelation 16:12

   b. The Sixth (6th) Vial
   1. The Euphrates River dried up.
      - Rivers have always been a hindrance to armies, but not as much so today as in the past.
      - England has been spared many times by the 20 miles of the English Channel.
      - One of Hitler's great mistakes in World War II was failing to destroy the bridge crossing the Rhine River.
   2. When God gets ready to destroy the beast and the kings of the earth and their armies at Armageddon, He will remove all obstacles by drying up the Euphrates River.
   3. The Euphrates is 1,780 miles long. It is from 300 to 1,200 yards wide, and 20 to 60 feet deep. Turkey has built a dam on the Euphrates and can cut off the water at any time.
   4. Who are the kings of the east?
      - Japan
      - China
      - Mongolia
      - India and all eastern Asia
   5. By the drying up of the Euphrates River, a passage is open for all nations east of Palestine to march westward toward Israel to Armageddon.

   c. Parenthetical – **vs. 13-16**
   1. *"[13] And I saw three unclean spirits like frogs come out of the mouth of the dragon, and out of the mouth of the beast, and out of the mouth of the false prophet. [14] For they are the spirits of devils, working miracles, which go forth unto the kings of the earth and of the whole world, to gather them to the battle of that great day of God*

Almighty. [15] Behold, I come as a thief. Blessed is he that watcheth, and keepeth his garments, lest he walk naked, and they see his shame. [16] And he gathered them together into a place called in the Hebrew tongue Armageddon." – Revelation 16:13-16

    2.   The Dragon – **vs. 13**
- Here we have the trinity of Hell
  - ❖ The Dragon – anti-God
  - ❖ The Beast – anti-Christ
  - ❖ The False Prophet – anti-Holy Spirit

    3.   The Dreadful Spirits – **vs. 13-16**
- When the Gospel is preached, there is One just behind the scene to bear the message to the heart; The Holy Spirit.
- Here in verses 13-16, there are evil spirits (demons) whispering into the hearts of the kings of the earth convincing them that they can fight against God and win. Their job is to gather the kings of the earth to the war of Armageddon. **(vs. 16)**
- Again, God faithfully sounds the warning. **(vs. 15)**

VII. **THE DESTRUCTION** – vs. 17-21

    a.   *"[17] And the seventh angel poured out his vial into the air; and there came a great voice out of the temple of heaven, from the throne, saying, It is done. [18] And there were voices, and thunders, and lightnings; and there was a great earthquake, such as was not since men were upon the earth, so mighty an earthquake, and so great. [19] And the great city was divided into three parts, and the cities of the nations fell: and great Babylon came in remembrance before God, to give unto her the cup of the wine of the fierceness of His wrath. [20] And every island fled away, and the mountains were not found. [21] And there fell upon men a great hail out of heaven, every stone about the weight of a talent: and men blasphemed God because of the plague of the hail; for the plague thereof was exceeding great."* – **Revelation 16:21**

- b. The Seventh (7th) Vial
  1. *"...It is done."* – **vs. 17**
     - A great voice, the voice of God, pierces the atmosphere from the throne of heaven proclaiming the finishing acts of *"Jacob's trouble"*. **(Jeremiah 30:7)**
     - The voice proclaims "It is done."
       - ❖ At Calvary, a cry "it is finished" – Christ's sufferings on the cross was finished.
       - ❖ Out of the Temple of heaven – "It is done" – The present age is finished.
  2. The shaking of the solar system – **vs. 18**
  3. The shaking of the earth – **vs. 18-20**
  4. The great city (Jerusalem) is divided – **vs. 19**
  5. Judgment on Babylon – **vs. 19 and Revelation 18**
  6. Great hail out of heaven fell upon men weighing 100 or more pounds – **vs. 21**
  7. The 7th vial carries us on to Revelation 19, Christ's Second Coming.

Revelation – Chapter 17

Religious Babylon – The Great Harlot

I. **THE DISGUSTING WOMAN – vs. 1**
   a. *"And there came one of the seven angels which had the seven vials, and talked with me, saying unto me, Come hither; I will shew unto thee the judgment of the great whore that sitteth upon many waters."* – Revelation 17:1
   b. This does not mean a new series of seven judgments, but rather, the seven vials of judgment wrath are God's final judgment on Babylon.
   c. God uses the figure of a harlot to describe an apostate false religious system.
   d. Spiritual unfaithfulness is spiritual adultery.
   e. This is the one world church of the last days. It has turned away from God. Such unbelief will become more and more intense as we near the end.
      1. **I Timothy 4:1**
      2. **II Timothy 3:1-5**
      3. **II Peter 2:1-2**
   f. The Destruction – **vs. 1**
      1. *"…Come hither; I will shew unto thee the judgment of the great whore…"* – **vs. 1**
      2. God has condemned the great prostitute who corrupted the earth by her adulteries. He has avenged on her the blood of His servants **(Revelation 19:2)**.
      3. God has already ordained her fall and judgment.
      4. Babylon is called the lady of kingdoms in **Isaiah 47:5**.

II. **THE DOMINATION – vs. 1-2**
   a. *"[1] And there came one of the seven angels which had the seven vials, and talked with me,*

saying unto me, Come hither; I will shew unto thee the judgment of the great whore that sitteth upon many waters. [2] With whom the kings of the earth have committed fornication, and the inhabitants of the earth have been made drunk with the wine of her fornication." – Revelation 17:2

    b.   Her Influence
- 1. We are told she *"sitteth upon many waters"*. – **vs. 1**
  - In verse 15, the waters are people, multitudes, nations, and tongues.
- 2. *"...the kings of the earth..."* – **vs. 2** -
  - Her influence is worldwide. People are swayed by her, to one degree or another.
- 3. We all know what adultery is. It is sexual immorality. Here the harlot has used sex and alcohol to entice and seduce world leaders spiritually and physically. She has pursued the same course of action with the rest of the population as well.

    c.   The Drunkenness – **vs. 2**
- 1. Here we have 2 things
  - Spiritual fornication and spiritual drunkenness.
  - Literal fornication and literal drunkenness will take place in the great tribulation.
  - These sins are rapidly increasing in our day and the judgment of God is rumbling in the distance.

III. <u>THE DESLOATION</u> – vs. 3

    a.   *"So he carried me away in the spirit into the wilderness: and I saw a woman sit upon a scarlet coloured beast, full of names of blasphemy, having seven heads and ten horns."* – Revelation 17:3

    b.   The wilderness is a sign of the chaotic condition of the world.
- 1. A desert is a waterless place
  - No preaching of the Gospel
- 2. A desert is a solitary place

- No witness
  - Dry place
  - No life
  - Place of desolation
  - Waste and barrenness
3. This is the condition of the apostate church. It powerfully reminds us that death, not life, is the environment in which she thrives best.
4. The animal is none other than the First Beast with seven heads and ten horns **(Revelation 13:1)**. Before he had the names of blasphemy on his heads; now he is full of blasphemy.
   - This shows us how sin continues to get worse and worse.
   - *"But evil men and seducers shall wax worse and worse, deceiving, and being deceived." –* II Timothy 3:13

IV. THE DECKED WOMAN – vs. 4
a. *"And the woman was arrayed in purple and scarlet colour, and decked with gold and precious stones and pearls, having a golden cup in her hand full of abominations and filthiness of her fornication:" –* **Revelation 17:4**
b. She has outward beauty.
   1. Arrayed in purple and scarlet color.
   2. She is like the Pharisees *"within full of dead men's bones, and full of all uncleanness". –* **Matthew 23:27**
c. She is rich.
   1. Gold
   2. Precious Stones
   3. Pearls
   4. She is like the Church at Laodicea, *"I am rich, and increased with goods, and have need of nothing;" –* **Revelation 3:17**
d. She is religious.
   1. John saw a cup in her hand made of gold, but full of her special dirty sins, attractive to men, but repulsive to God."

V. THE DESCRIPTION – vs. 5

a. *"And upon her forehead was a name written, MYSTERY BABYLON THE GREAT, THE MOTHER OF HARLOTS AND ABOMINATIONS OF THE EARTH." –* **Revelation 17:5**
b. The word mystery is one of the names of the woman. Paul had written of the mystery of iniquity **(II Thessalonians 2:7)**.
c. All false religions came from Babylon.
d. Being the mother of harlots, she is the source of all apostate groups whose heart go out to her false doctrine and idolatry. She will be, in fact, the counterfeit of the New Jerusalem.

VI. THE DESTRUCTION – vs. 6

a. *"And I saw the woman drunken with the blood of the saints, and with the blood of the martyrs of Jesus: and when I saw her, I wondered with great admiration." –* **Revelation 17:6**
b. The cry of the religious world today is to be tolerant. But, when opportunity and the power are available, false religion will not tolerate anyone who will not submit to its belief. She destroys everything in her path that opposes her **(Revelation 13:15)**.
c. John viewed the woman with great admiration. Not that he admired her conquest with respect, but with great admiration seeing the great number of martyrs, he marveled at the sight.

VII. THE DECLARATION – vs. 7

a. *"And the angel said unto me, Wherefore didst thou marvel? I will tell thee the mystery of the woman, and of the beast that carrieth her, which hath the seven heads and ten horns." –* **Revelation 17:7**
b. In **Ephesians 5**, we have the mystery of Christ and the Church. Now the angel is going to reveal to John, and through him, and to us the mystery of the woman and the beast." – **Revelation 17:8**

REVELATION—CHAPTER 17

The Last Form of Gentile World Power

I. THE BEAST (The anti-Christ) – vs. 8
  a. *"The beast that thou sawest was, and is not; and shall ascend out of the bottomless pit, and go into perdition: and they that dwell on the earth shall wonder, whose names were not written in the book of life from the foundation of the world, when they behold the beast that was, and is not, and yet is."* – Revelation 17:8
  b. *"The beast that thou sawest..."* – vs. 8
    1. One who has lived.
  c. *"...and is not..."* – vs. 8
    1. Was dead in John's time.
  d. *"...and yet is."* – vs. 8
    1. Would be resurrected in the future – **Revelation 13:3**
  e. *"...bottomless pit..."* – vs. 8
    1. The beast ascends out of the bottomless pit and out of Satan's incarnate son of perdition. – **II Thessalonians 2:3**
  f. *"...book of life..."* – vs. 8
    1. Everyone, except those whose names were in the book of life, admired him (the anti-Christ).
    2. For details regarding the book of life, refer back to **Revelation 3:5**.

II. THE WISDOM – vs. 9-13
  a. *"[9] And here is the mind which hath wisdom. The seven heads are seven mountains, on which the woman sitteth. [10] And there are seven kings: five are fallen, and one is, and the other is not yet come; and when he cometh, he must continue a short space. [11] And the beast that was, and is not, even he is the eighth, and is of the seven, and goeth into perdition, [12] And the ten horns which thou sawest are ten kings, which have received no kingdom as yet; but receive power as kings one hour with the beast. [13]*

              These have one mind, and shall give their power and strength unto the beast." – Revelation 17:9-13
- b. Here is the true revelation concerning the beast and the woman. – **vs. 9**
   1. Here is the mind which hath wisdom
   2. We should have the mind of the Holy Spirit and not be ignorant.
   3. Here, mountains are symbolic of kingdoms.
- c. Verse 10 tells us the seven heads are seven kings. Some believe these seven heads were the seven different forms of governments, which Rome passed through. Others see these seven kings as the seven world empires of Egypt, Assyria, Babylon, Medo-Persia, and Greece. These five have already fallen.
   1. I believe the seven heads refer to the seven world empires is the correct view of this.
- d. "One is", is the Roman Empire which was ruling in John's day. "The other is not yet come" will be the kingdom of the anti-Christ. When he has come, he must continue a short space.
   1. The short space is the last half (3½) years of the seven year tribulation.
   2. The anti-Christ will have complete control of the world. – **Revelation 13:3-5**
- e. Verse 11 is the resurrection of the beast (the anti-Christ) and takes us back to **Revelation 13:3**.
- f. *"...he is the eighth, and is of the seven..."* – **vs. 11**
   1. The beast comes out of the seven, thus he is called the eighth.
   2. He will rise out of one of these historical kingdoms.
- g. This empire has 10 kings that rule with the beast for a short time. They give the beast all of their support. – **vs. 12-13**

III. <u>THE WAR</u> – vs. 14
- a. *"These shall make war with the Lamb, and the Lamb shall overcome them: for He is Lord of lords, and King of kings: and they that are with him are called, and chosen, and faithful."* – **Revelation 17:14**

     b.   The purpose of the beast's empire is to make war with the Lamb. The Lamb overcomes them.
          1.   "These" here in this verse are the 10 kings or kingdoms.
          2.   The Lamb is Christ.
     c.   ***"…He is Lord of lords…" – vs. 14***
          1.   This speaks of His deity.
     d.   ***"…King of kings…" – vs. 14***
          1.   This speaks of His humanity.
     e.   ***"…they that are with him are called, and chosen, and faithful." – vs. 14***
          1.   The Godly believers who are called, and chosen, and faithful, will share in Christ's victorious conquest. They will share with Him in His moment of glory.
          2.   These believers are the "tribulation saints", or those who have been saved during the tribulation time.
          3.   What a thrilling statement of intent for the people of God.

IV.   THE WHORE – vs. 15

     a.   ***"And he saith unto me, The waters which thou sawest, where the whore sitteth, are peoples, and multitudes, and nations, and tongues." – Revelation 17:15***
     b.   Her influence and wealth.
          1.   ***"…peoples, and multitudes, and nations, and tongues." – vs. 15***
          2.   The prostitute is controlling them.
          3.   Also, they persecute God's people just as all false religions do.

V.   THE WILL OF GOD – vs. 16-17

     a.   ***"[16] And the ten horns which thou sawest upon the beast, these shall hate the whore, and shall make her desolate and naked, and shall eat her flesh, and burn her with fire. [17] For God hath put in their hearts to fulfil His will, and to agree,*** and give their kingdom unto the beast, until the words of God shall be fulfilled."* – **Revelation 17:16-17**

- b. *"...the ten horns..."* – **vs. 16**
    1. These represent the political side of the revived Roman Empire.
- c. *"...these shall hate the whore..."* – **vs. 16**
    1. The political side of the Roman Empire makes a split from the religious side of the empire.
- d. *"...and shall make her desolate and naked..."* – **vs. 16**
    1. They will awaken from their drunken stupor with the woman, whose charm and seduction will have lost their lure.
    2. They will make her desolate or deprive her of all the wealth she has confiscated.
    3. They will make her naked, stripping away her personal support, position, power, and prestige, and thus exposing her moral corruption.
- e. *"...shall eat her flesh, and burn her with fire."* – **vs. 16**
    1. Love for the woman will turn to hate.
    2. They shall eat her flesh like wild dogs devoured the corpse of Jezebel – **I Kings 21:23, II Kings 9:30-37**
    3. They burn her with fire, totally eliminating any identity of the woman and her false religious system.
        - Israel's law required that those who committed extreme acts of sin be burned with fire after their deaths to remove any symbol of their remembrance. – **Leviticus 20:14; 21:9, Joshua 7:15-25**
    4. Just before the midpoint of the tribulation, the 10 kings along with the beast will destroy her.
- f. *"For God hath put in their hearts to fulfil His will, and to agree, and give their kingdom unto the beast, until the words of God shall be fulfilled."* – **vs. 17**
    1. Notice whose will is being done. God's will.

REVELATION—CHAPTER 17

2. This verse explains how God will be behind the fall of Religious Babylon in that He will put in the hearts of the kings to fulfill His will and to agree and give their kingdoms unto the beast until the words of God be fulfilled.
3. God can use any instrument He wills to carry out His purpose. The Assyrian of old was God's rod on Samaria **(Isaiah 10:5-19)**.
4. The beast and the ten kings in this chapter, though hating and blaspheming God, are His tools, without knowledge or will of their own, to accomplish His unfailing purpose.

VI. <u>**THE WOMAN**</u> – vs. 18
    a. *"And the woman which thou sawest is that great city, which reigneth over the kings of the earth."* – **Revelation 17:18**
    b. This is the end of the apostate Church of whom the woman is a symbol.
    c. The political system shall destroy the religious system.

Revelation – Chapter 18

Political Babylon

In Chapter 17, we studied about religious Babylon and her doom. The 10 kings hate the whore and burn her with fire. Three and one-half years later, political Babylon is destroyed by God.

I. **THE POWERFUL ANGEL – vs. 1**
   a. *"And after these things I saw another angel come down from heaven, having great power; and the earth was lightened with his glory." –* **Revelation 18:1**
   b. This angel comes down from heaven having great power to perform an act of judgment, such as never been known before, upon Babylon.
   c. The angel has great authority and the earth is lightened with his glory. This tells us that God is on the scene.

II. **THE PRESUMPTUOUS CITY – vs. 2**
   a. *"And he cried mightily with a strong voice, saying, Babylon the great is fallen, is fallen, and is become the habitation of devils, and the hold of every foul spirit, and a cage of every unclean and hateful bird." –* **Revelation 18:2**
   b. Babylon becomes bold and forward in her sins. She overstepped the bounds of God's mercy. The powerful angel cries saying, *"Babylon the great is fallen, is fallen"*.
      1. She *"...is become the habitation of devils." –* vs. 2
         • Demon worship
      2. *"...and the hold of every foul spirit..." –* vs. 2
         • The spirit of the world

❖ The spirit of disobedience – **Ephesians 2:2**
❖ The spirit of error – **I John 4:6**
3. *"...a cage of every unclean and hateful bird." – vs. 2*
- Symbolic of Satan and his demons – **Matthew 13:3-4**

III. THE PROSPEROUS CITY – vs. 3
a. *"For all nations have drunk of the wine of the wrath of her fornication, and the kings of the earth have committed fornication with her, and the merchants of the earth are waxed rich through the abundance of her delicacies." – Revelation 18:3*
b. Babylon's wealth will attract the world's commerce to herself. She has seduced the nations from their belief in God and Christ. She has established herself in the affections of the masses of mankind.
c. At this period of time, the Bible will be dethroned from its place in public and from the conscience of the masses, even of the religious world.
d. The nations have drunk of her cup and have become intoxicated with her sins and riches, and no longer has power to resist her.

IV. THE PLEA – vs. 4
a. *"And I heard another voice from heaven, saying, Come out of her, my people, that ye be not partakers of her sins, and that ye receive not of her plagues." – Revelation 18:4*
b. A call to separation is addressed to the tribulation saints of that day. However, it is a warning to believers today who, even now, discern the rising tide of iniquity.

V. THE REMEMBERANCE – vs. 5
a. *"For her sins have reached unto heaven, and God hath remembered her iniquities." – Revelation 18:5*

EPISODES OF THE END, THE REVELATION OF JESUS CHRIST

    b.   The first Babel tried to build a tower to heaven. – **Genesis 11:4**
    c.   The last Babel heaped up her sins to heaven. Now they have built an empire of sin that reached unto heaven.
        1.   It may seem that God has forgotten and is silent. Judgment may slumber long, but suddenly God acts and the end is terrible.

VI. THE REWARD – vs. 6
    a.   *"Reward her even as she rewarded you, and double unto her double according to her works: in the cup which she hath filled fill to her double."* – **Revelation 18:6**
    b.   Reaping time has come.
    c.   Babylon has filled her cup to the double, and now she must reap the same.
        1.   Babylon's punishment will be doubled for the evil that she has done to the saints.

VII. THE RETRIBUTION – vs. 7-8
    a.   *"[7] How much she hath glorified herself, and lived deliciously, so much torment and sorrow give her: for she saith in her heart, I sit a queen, and am no widow, and shall see no sorrow. [8] Therefore shall her plagues come in one day, death, and mourning, and famine; and she shall be utterly burned with fire: for strong is the Lord God who judgeth her."* – **Revelation 18:7-8**
    b.   She was actively glorifying herself and living in luxury.
        1.   Her self glorification will lead to self sufficiency and self deification (deifying), meaning "to make a god".
        2.   She has made herself her own god; the final self deception.
    c.   Because of her pride and willful sin against God, her judgment comes in one day **(vs. 8)**, and in one hour **(vs. 10, 17, 19)**.
        1.   In a single day, she will be gone.

        2. Actually, verses 10, 17, and 19, implies it will be over within 60 minutes.
- d. The plagues are:
  1. Death – **Revelation 18:8**
  2. Mourning – **Revelation 18:8**
  3. Famine – **Revelation 18:8**

VIII. THE MOURNING – vs. 9
- a. *"And the kings of the earth, who have committed fornication and lived deliciously with her, shall bewail her, and lament for her, when they shall see the smoke of her burning,"* – Revelation 18:9
- b. The kings lead in mourning since they profited most by Babylon's world-wide commercial influence.

IX. THE MASTER STROKE – vs. 10
- a. *"Standing afar off for the fear of her torment, saying, Alas, alas, that great city of Babylon, that mighty city! For in one hour is thy judgment come."* – Revelation 18:10
- b. *"...For in one hour is thy judgment come."* – vs. 10
  1. *"He that being often reproved hardeneth his neck, shall suddenly be destroyed, and that without remedy."* – Proverbs 29:1
  2. *"For when they shall say, Peace and safety; then sudden destruction cometh upon them, as travail upon a woman with child; and they shall not escape."* – I Thessalonians 5:3
  3. "**In one hour**", in one unexpected, unanticipated hour, God's righteous judgment fell in suddenness **(vs. 8, 17, 19)**.

X. THE MERCHANTS AND MERCHANDISE – vs. 11-19
- a. *"[11] And the merchants of the earth shall weep and mourn over her; for no man buyeth their merchandise any more: [12] The merchandise of*

gold, and silver, and precious stones, and of pearls, and fine linen, and purple, and silk, and scarlet, and all thyine wood, and all manner vessels of ivory, and all manner vessels of most precious wood, and of brass, and iron, and marble, [13] And cinnamon, and odours, and ointments, and frankincense, and wine, and oil, and fine flour, and wheat, and beasts, and sheep, and horses, and chariots, and slaves, and souls of men. [14] And the fruits that thy soul lusteth after are departed from thee, and all things which were dainty and goodly are departed from thee, and thou shalt find them no more at all. [15] The merchants of these things which were made rich by her, shall stand afar off for the fear of her torment, weeping and wailing, [16] And saying, Alas, alas that great city, that was clothed in fine linen, and purple, and scarlet, and decked with gold, and precious stones, and pearls! [17] For in one hour so great riches is come to nought. And every shipmaster, and all the company in ships, and sailors, and as many as trade by sea, stood afar off, [18] And cried when they saw the smoke of her burning, saying, What city is like unto this great city! [19] And they cast dust on their heads, and cried, weeping and wailing, saying, Alas, alas that great city, wherein were made rich all that had ships in the sea by reason of her costliness! For in one hour is she made desolate." – Revelation 18:11-19

    b.   Riches cannot save.
           1.   *"He that trusteth in his riches shall fall: but the righteous shall flourish as a branch."* – Proverbs 11:28
           2.   *"Wilt thou set thine eyes upon that which is not? For riches certainly make themselves wings; they fly away as an eagle toward heaven."* – Proverbs 23:5
    c.   The commodities fell into eight categories – **vs. 12-13**
           1.   Precious metals
- Gold
- Silver

- Precious stones
- Pearls
2. Costly Clothing
   - Fine linen
   - Purple
   - Silk
   - Scarlet
3. Materials for Furniture
   - Wood
   - Ivory
4. Vessels
   - Wood
   - Bronze
   - Iron
   - Marble
5. Perfumes
   - Cinnamon
   - Odours
   - Ointments
   - Frankincense
6. Food
   - Wine
   - Oil
   - Flour
   - Wheat
   - Beasts
   - Sheep
7. Conveyances
   - Horses
   - Chariots
8. Slaves and souls of men
   - Notice here that slavery is still in existence in the tribulation.

d. The Loss of Merchandise – **vs. 14**
   1. **"And the fruits that thy soul lusteth after are departed from thee... thou shalt find them no more at all." – vs. 14**
   2. Riches, position, and leadership vanished overnight in this collapse.

e. The Lamentation of the Merchants and the Mariners (Sailors) – **vs. 15-19**

                1. *"...weeping and wailing..."* – **vs. 15**
                    - We see people of wealth losing their entire fortunes in one day. – **vs. 16**
                    - This is the collapse of transportation in the tribulation. This includes trucks, planes, ships, and rail systems. – **vs. 17**
                    - International trade is over. – **vs. 17**
                    - ***"And cried when they saw the smoke of her burning..."* – vs. 18**
                2. They trusted in the power of the system, and now it has fallen and they watch and cry in amazement.
        f. Their Livelihood Gone – **vs. 19**
                1. *"...For in one hour is she made desolate."* – **vs. 19**
                    - Cargo ships are out of business.
                    - Riches go up in judgment.
                2. Three worlds enriched by Babylon
                    - Governmental world – **Revelation 18:9-10**
                    - Commercial world – **Revelation 18:11-16**
                    - Maritime world – **Revelation 18:17-19**

XI. <u>THE REJOICING</u> – vs. 20
   a. *"Rejoice over her, thou heaven, and ye holy apostles and prophets; for God hath avenged you on her."* – **Revelation 18:20**
   b. While the merchants and kings, and sailors weep, the saints in heaven rejoice over the destruction of Babylon. The cause is clear, **"God hath avenged you on her".** – **vs. 20**
        1. *"...Vengeance is Mine; I will repay, saith the Lord."* – **Romans 12:19**
        2. The saints in heaven rejoice as God avenges His own.
   c. Payday has come. Here we see God's attitude toward sin.

REVELATION—CHAPTER 18

XII. **THE REAPING – vs. 21-23**
    a. *"[21] And a mighty angel took up a stone like a great millstone, and cast it into the sea, saying, Thus with violence shall that great city Babylon be thrown down, and shall be found no more at all. [22] And the voice of harpers, and musicians, and of pipers, and trumpeters, shall be heard no more at all in thee; and no craftsman, of whatsoever craft he be, shall be found any more in thee; and the sound of a millstone shall be heard no more at all in thee; [23] And the light of a candle shall shine no more at all in thee; and the voice of the bridegroom and of the bride shall be heard no more at all in thee: for thy merchants were the great men of the earth; for by thy sorceries were all nations deceived." – Revelation 18:21-23*
    b. They sowed to the wind and they reaped the whirlwind.
        1. *"For they have sown the wind, and they shall reap the whirlwind:..."* **– Hosea 8:7**
    c. Like the boulder in the ocean, she has gone down under. She will never reappear in any shape or form. This is it! She is finished. End of the line. Nothing more will be written about her. She has come and she has gone. **– vs. 21**
        1. City and system in desolation **– vs. 22**
- No music
- No harpers
- No musicians
- No pipers
- No trumpeters
- No manufacturing
- No craftsman
- No industry

        2. Drugs and deception **– vs. 23**
- *"...the light of a candle..."* **– vs. 23**
  - ❖ Refers to the entertainment world falling apart.
- *"...the voice of the bridegroom..."* **– vs. 23**

- ❖ Refers to all social activity coming apart.
- *"...the bride shall be heard no more..."* – vs. 23
  - ❖ Refers to no more celebrations.
- *"...for by thy sorceries were all nations deceived..."* – vs. 23
  - ❖ The word sorceries means one who abuses and becomes addicted to drugs.
  - ❖ The anti-Christ will use drugs as one of his means to deceive the world.

XIII. THE REVELATION – vs. 24
    a.   *"And in her was found the blood of prophets, and of saints, and of all that were slain upon the earth."* – Revelation 18:24
    b.   This reveals the hatred of these religious leaders.
    c.   They slaughter God's saints.

Revelation – Chapter 19

Note the difference in spelling the word Alleluia or Hallelujah. This comes from the fact that in the Hebrew language they have the letter "H", but in the Greek language, they do not.

The Four Alleluias

I. **THE FIRST ALLELUIA – vs. 1**
    a.   *"And after these things I heard a great voice of much people in heaven, saying, Alleluia; Salvation, and glory, and honour, and power, unto the Lord our God:"* – Revelation 19:1
    b.   The Shout of Redemption
        1.   Alleluia means, "praise the Lord". It is the same in all languages. It is a universal word. It occurs many times in the Old Testament, especially in Psalms. It is used only four times in the New Testament **(Revelation 19:1-6)**.
        2.   The saved in heaven praise God for:
- Salvation
- Glory
- Honour
- Power

II. **THE SECOND ALLELUIA – vs. 2-3**
    a.   *"[2] For true and righteous are His judgment: for He hath judged the great whore, which did corrupt the earth with her fornication, and hath avenged the blood of His servants at her hand. [3] And again, they said, Alleluia. And her smoke rose up for ever and ever."* – Revelation 19:2-3
    b.   The Shout of Retribution
        1.   They shout because of God's judgment upon the great harlot.

III. THE THIRD ALLELUIA – vs. 4-5
a. *"[4] And the four and twenty elders and the four beasts fell down and worshipped God that sat on the throne, saying, Amen; Alleluia. [5] And a voice came out of the throne, saying, Praise our God, all ye His servants, and ye that fear Him, both small and great."* – Revelation 19:4-5
b. The Shout of Realization
   1. It is in recognition of obedience to God. In fact, when they bow before Him, it is a meaningful tribute to the sovereignty of the One who is King of kings and Lord of lords.
   2. The phrase *"His servants, and ye that fear Him, both small and great"* refers not to a specific group, but to all of the servants in heaven. – **vs. 5**
   3. They are encouraged to continue praising God for His mighty victory, no matter what their status.

IV. THE FOURTH ALLELUIA – vs. 6
a. *"And I heard as it were the voice of a great multitude, and as the voice of many waters, and as the voice of mighty thunderings, saying, Alleluia: for the Lord God omnipotent reigneth."* – Revelation 19:6
b. The Shout of Christ's Reign
   1. Christ is about to set up His kingdom and rule the world with a rod of iron **(Psalm 2:9, Revelation 2:27)** for 1000 years **(Revelation 20:1-9)**.
   2. The saints shout Alleluia. Their praise will reverberate through heaven like the voice of many waters and mighty peals of thunder.
   3. The sound coming from the host of heaven will be deafening like the noise of a mighty waterfall and the booming of thunder echoing throughout the sky.

REVELATION—CHAPTER 19

| The Marriage of the Lamb |

V. THE FINALIZATION – vs. 7
    a.   *"Let us be glad and rejoice, and give honour to Him: for the marriage of the Lamb is come, and His wife hath made herself ready."* – **Revelation 19:7**
    b.   The marriage of the Lamb is come.
    c.   There are three stages to an oriental wedding:
        1.   The engagement
           • It will last at least one (1) year.
        2.   The wedding itself
           • The marriage ceremony
        3.   The wedding reception
           • The marriage supper
    d.   The Church in her relationship to Christ will go through all three stages.
        1.   The Church is now
           • Engaged to Christ – **II Corinthians 11:2**
           • She will one day be united to Him when He comes for her. – **John 14:2**
           • She will join in the marriage supper of the Lamb – **Revelation 19:9**

VI. THE FINE LINEN – vs. 8
    a.   *"And to her was granted that she should be arrayed in fine linen, clean and white: for the fine linen is the righteousness of saints."* – **Revelation 19:8**
    b.   The bride is the bride because of the righteousness of Christ.
    c.   The bride is clothed for the wedding because of her acts.
    d.   The linen is said to be the righteousness of the saints.
        1.   The fine linen is a rewarded righteousness.
    e.   His wife has made herself ready.
        1.   The saints will appear before the Judgment Seat of Christ – **Romans 14:10, II Corinthians 5:10**

        2.   This judgment is not to determine if we are saved or lost, but for rewards. We will either be rewarded or suffer loss, depending on what kind of works we have. – **I Corinthians 3:10-15**

VII. <u>THE FRIENDS OR GUESTS</u> – vs. 9
    a.   *"And he saith unto me, Write, Blessed are they which are called unto the marriage supper of the Lamb. And he saith unto me, These are the true sayings of God."* – **Revelation 19:9**
    b.   Who are those *"called unto the marriage support of the Lamb"*?
        1.   The invitation is given to Old Testament saints, Martyred Tribulation Saints, believers who survive the tribulation, and John the Baptist who is a friend of the bridegroom **(John 3:29)**.

VIII. <u>THE FELLOWSERVANT</u> – vs. 10
    a.   *"And I fell at his feet to worship him. And he said unto me, See thou do it not: I am thy fellow servant, and of thy brethren that have the testimony of Jesus: worship God: for the testimony of Jesus is the spirit of prophecy."* – **Revelation 19:10**
    b.   The misplaced worship of the angel by John.
        1.   Angels are not objects of worship, neither men nor any other creature.
- **Revelation 22:8-9**
- **Acts 10:25-26**
- **Matthew 4:10**
- **Colossians 1:18**

        2.   God is to be worshipped, and God only, in spirit and truth.
- **John 4:24**
- **Acts 12:20-23**

REVELATION—CHAPTER 19

> The Second Coming of Christ

IX. **<u>THE FAITHFUL AND TRUE CHRIST</u> – vs. 11-16**
   a. *"[11] And I saw heaven opened, and behold a white horse; and He that sat upon him was called Faithful and True, and in righteousness He doth judge and make war. [12] His eyes were as a flame of fire, and on His head were many crowns; and He had a name written, that no man knew, but He Himself. [13] And He was clothed with a vesture dipped in blood: and His name is called The Word of God. [14] And the armies which were in heaven followed Him upon white horses, clothed in fine linen, white and clean. [15] And out of His mouth goeth a sharp sword, that with it He should smite the nations: and He shall rule them with a rod of iron: and He treadeth the winepress of the fierceness and wrath of Almighty God. [16] And He hath on His vesture and on His thigh a name written KING OF KINGS, AND LORD OF LORDS."* – **Revelation 19:11-16**
   b. Christ rides from the open heaven on a white horse – **vs. 11**
      1. Why is Christ on a white horse?
         - The white horse represents purity and victory.
      2. He is called Faithful and True – **vs. 11**
         - He is faithful in that He will do all that He has promised.
         - He is true, in contrast to all false Christ's.
         - Christ will judge in righteousness and make righteous war.
      3. *"…He doth judge…"* – **vs. 11**
         - Christ will judge every unbeliever.
   c. The Description of His glorious person continues – **vs. 12**
      1. His eyes indicate penetration, scrutinizing, and omniscience (all knowing).
      2. *"…on His head many crowns…"* – **vs. 12**
         - He is supreme authority.

EPISODES OF THE END, THE REVELATION OF JESUS CHRIST

- He has passed from a crown of thorns, a crown of humiliation and derision, to the crowned King of kings and Lord of lords.
- He is a King come to judge the world.

3. The name which no man knew is just that, unrevealed.

d. Christ does not come to save but to judge – **vs. 13**
1. At the Lord's first coming, **"the Father sent the Son to be the Saviour of the world" (I John 4:14)**.
2. Evident in His second coming will be the fact that **"...the Father judgeth no man, but hath committed all judgment unto the Son...and hath given Him authority to execute judgment also, because His is the Son of Man" (John 5:22, 27)**.
3. It is necessary to remember that God is love and God is righteous. Men who have refused His love will have to face His righteous judgments. The Son of God reveals both sides of God's character.

e. The Armies from Heaven – **vs. 14**
1. Who are the armies in the fine linen on the white horses?
2. It appears they are:
   - Church Saints – **Revelation 19:8**
   - Tribulation Saints – **Revelation 6:9-11**
   - Angels – **Matthew 25:31**
   - Old Testament Saints
     ❖ **Jude 14-15** will then be fulfilled.

f. The Sharp Sword – **vs. 15**
1. The sharp sword is the Word of God. – **Isaiah 11:4**
2. But, specifically in judgment, the nations, the object of His rule will be ruled with a rod of iron. – **Psalm 2:9 – Revelation 12:5**
3. The word rule means "a shepherd".
4. He will rule in perfect discipline and perfect justice.
5. There are 3 symbols of judgment in verse 15:
   - A sharp sword for immediate, judicial punishment, probably death.

- A rod for righteous, inflexible government.
- The winepress of wrath for the guiltiest of all.
  - ❖ The latter is the expression of the most extreme wrath.

g. His Name – **vs. 16**
1. King of kings
   - This refers to His humanity.
2. Lord of Lords
   - This refers to His deity.
3. The answer to Pilate's mocking question, ***"Art Thou a king then?"* (John 18:37)**, is now given from heaven; ***"KING OF KINGS, AND LORD OF LORDS"* (Revelation 19:16)**.
4. Paul wrote in anticipation, ***"...He shall shew who is the blessed and only Potentate (ruler), the King of kings, and Lord of lords"* (I Timothy 6:15)**.
5. The angel in **Revelation 17:14** identified the same moment: ***"...and the Lamb shall overcome them: for He is Lord of lords, and King of kings:...".***
6. Moses, in **Deuteronomy 10:17**, and Nebuchadnezzar, in **Daniel 2:47**, spoke of deity in these terms. But now it is manifest in Christ and He is the absolute sovereign.

The Battle of Armageddon

X. **THE FOWLS AND THE FEAST** – vs. 17-19

a. *"[17] And I saw an angel standing in the sun; and he cried with a loud voice, saying to all the fowls that fly in the midst of heaven, Come and gather yourselves together unto the supper of the great God; [18] That ye may eat the flesh of kings, and the flesh of captains, and the flesh of mighty men, and the flesh of horses, and of them that sit on them, and the flesh of all men, both free and bond, both small and great. [19] And I saw the beast, and the kings of the earth, and their armies gathered together to make war against Him that sat on the horse, and against His army."* – **Revelation 19:17-19**

    b.   The angel invites the fowls to Armageddon – **vs. 17**
        1.   The fowls feast on the flesh of captains, mighty men, horses, of all men both free and bond, both small and great.
        2.   Armageddon means "mount of slaughter".
        3.   God prepares a supper of ghastly, grief, and gloom which stands in sharp contrast to the gladness and joy of the marriage supper of the Lamb.
- The supper of delight – **vs. 9**
  - Marriage Supper of the Lamb
- The supper of destruction – **vs. 17-18**
  - Armageddon

The Doom of the Beast

XI. THE FORWARD BEAST (Anti-Christ) AND THE FALSE PROPHET – vs. 19-20

    a.   *"[19] And I saw the beast, and the kings of the earth, and their armies gathered together to make war against Him that sat on the horse, and against His army. [20] And the beast was taken, and with him the false prophet that wrought miracles before him, with which he deceived them that had received the mark of the beast, and them that worshipped his image. These both were cast alive into a lake of fire burning with brimstone."* – **Revelation 19:19-20**

    b.   The beast and the false prophet and their followers, the kings of the earth and their armies, defy God right up to the very last. God cast the beast and the false prophet alive into the lake of fire. The people whom the false prophet deceived await the final judgment of the unsaved before the Great White Throne which is 1000 years later. – **Revelation 20:11-15**

    c.   They have had:
        1.   Their say

2. Their way
3. Their day
d. The anti-Christ and the false prophet have the rare honor, if you want to call it that, of being the first two who are cast into the lake of fire. Even the devil is not there yet. It is over for them.
e. The anti-Christ, who is probably the greatest intellectual, the greatest politician, the greatest statesman, the greatest economist, who ever lived becomes the greatest fool when he tries to mastermind a quick one over the Lord Jesus Christ.

The Doom of the Kings

XII. THE FILLING OF THE FOWLS – vs. 21
a. ***"And the remnant were slain with the sword of Him that sat upon the horse, which sword proceeded out of His mouth: and all the fowls were filled with their flesh."*** – Revelation 19:21
b. Another Word, and the massed troops from all around the world fall down dead.
c. Not one person escapes. It all happens so quickly, no one can jump ship or change sides. There is no time to hoist the white flag of surrender.
d. The bodies of the slain will not decay. The fowls will fill themselves with their flesh.
e. What a horrible scene.
1. ***"...the wages of sin is death..."*** – Romans 6:23

Revelation – Chapter 20

The Binding of Satan and The Reign of Christ

The Binding of Satan

I. **THE BINDING OF SATAN** – vs. 1-3
   a. *"[1] And I saw an angel come down from heaven, having the key of the bottomless pit and a great chain in his hand. [2] And He laid hold on the dragon, that old serpent, which is the Devil, and Satan, and bound him a thousand years, [3] And cast him into the bottomless pit, and shut him up, and set a seal upon him, that he should deceive the nations no more, till the thousand years should be fulfilled: and after that he must be loosed a little season."* – **Revelation 20:1-3**
   b. Satan, who for millenniums, has been deceiving, devouring, and destroying the souls of mankind. He will be bound and cast into the bottomless pit for 1000 years.
   c. What man has failed to do, Christ will do; rule this world for 1000 years in righteousness and peace.
   d. At the end of the 1000 years, Satan is loosed for a little season. – **Revelation 20:7**
       a. Dragon – indicates cruelty – **vs. 2**
       b. Serpent – speaks of deception – **vs. 2**
       c. Devil – tempter of man – **vs. 2**
       d. Satan – adversary of Christ and His people – **vs. 2**

The First Resurrection (I Corinthians 15:52) and the Thousand Year Reign

REVELATION—CHAPTER 20

II. <u>THE BELOVED COMPANY</u> – vs. 4-5

    a.   *"[4] And I saw thrones, and they sat upon them, and judgment was given unto them: and I saw the souls of them that were beheaded for the witness of Jesus, and for the word of God, and which had not worshipped the beast, neither his image, neither had received his mark upon their foreheads, or in their hands; and they lived and reigned with Christ a thousand years. [5] But the rest of the dead lived not again until the thousand years were finished. This is the first resurrection."* **– Revelation 20:4-5**

    b.   Two Classes of Saints
        1.   Church Saints
- *"And I saw thrones, and they sat upon them, and judgment was given unto them:"* – vs. 4
- Paul tells us in **I Corinthians 6:2** that the saints shall judge the world. This refers to the millennial and eternal reign of Christ with His saints.
- They will reign over all nations on the earth and help administer the affairs of the universe.
  - ❖ **Isaiah 9:6-7**
  - ❖ **Daniel 7:13-14, 27**
  - ❖ **Zechariah 14:9-21**
  - ❖ **Matthew 19:28**
  - ❖ **Revelation 11:15**
  - ❖ **Revelation 20:4**
  - ❖ **Revelation 22:5**
- Also in **I Corinthians 6:3**, Paul tells us we shall judge angels. The word judge means to judge, to distinguish, or make a legal decision. It does not refer to passing sentence on angels or sending them to punishment. It does mean that saints will be exalted higher than the angels and will rule them. The saints, not angels, become the heirs of God and joint heirs with Jesus to inherit all things.
  - ❖ **Romans 8:17**

- ❖ **Hebrews 6:12**
- ❖ **Revelation 21:7**
- Even now, saints are being examples to angels **(I Corinthians 4:9)**. Angels are eager to learn about the plan of God for the redeemed **(I Peter 1:12)**.

2. Tribulation Saints
   - *"...I saw the souls of them that were beheaded for the witness of Jesus, and for the word of God..."* – vs. 4
   - These are tribulation martyrs.
   - In **Revelation 6:9-11** we have the early tribulation martyrs. Here in verse 4, we have the latter tribulation martyrs. They did not receive the mark of the beast, and did not worship the beast or his image.
   - *"...they lived and reigned with Christ for a thousand years."* – vs. 4
     - ❖ At the beginning of the 1000 year reign of Christ, there is a resurrection of the tribulation saints. These are the ones who were martyred for the cause of Christ.
   - *"But the rest of the dead lived not again until the thousand years were finished."* – vs. 5
     - ❖ These are the unsaved. They are in hell.
     - ❖ A 1000 years separate the resurrection of the just and the unjust.

III. THE BLESSED OF THE FIRST RESURRECTION – vs. 6

   a. *"Blessed and holy is he that hath part in the first resurrection: on such the second death had no power, but they shall be priests of God and of Christ, and shall reign with Him a thousand years."* – **Revelation 20:6**
   b. Christ is the first fruits of them that slept. – **I Corinthians 15:20**

    c.   Also, in the first resurrection there will be others.
          1.   ***"Christ, the first fruits, afterward they that are Christ's, at His coming." –* I Corinthians 15:23**
          2.   This is the rapture of the Church.
    d.   At the beginning of the kingdom age, we see other Saints, tribulation martyrs who were beheaded and killed. They are said to be part of the first resurrection **(Revelation 20:4, 6)**.
    e.   Blessed means "supremely blest" or "happy".
          1.   All saints are blessed.
          2.   This comes by God's:
- Grace – **Ephesians 2:8**
- Love – **John 3:16**
- Mercy – **Titus 3:5**

Satan Loosed: The Doom of Gog and Magog

IV. **THE DEPARTURE, DECEPTION, AND DEPRAVITY** – vs. 7-8

    a.   ***"[7] And when the thousand years are expired, Satan shall be loosed out of his prison, [8] And shall go out to deceive the nations which are in the four quarters of the earth, Gog and Magog, to gather them together to battle: the number of whom is as the sand of the sea." –* Revelation 20:7-8**
    b.   Satan is loosed from the pit to test the secrets of men's hearts. – **vs. 7**
    c.   He deceives the nations. – **vs. 8**
          1.   He is the arch deceiver. He knows exactly what to do.
          2.   He has plotted his revenge for a 1000 years.
          3.   He finds a following. – **vs. 8**
    d.   Some will escape death in the tribulation and will enter the millennium (1000 years) in their natural bodies and will have children. – **Isaiah 65:20**
    e.   The rebels follow Satan. This shows the depravity of man's heart.

V. THE DESTRUCTION – vs. 9

    a. *"And they went up on the breadth of the earth, and compassed the camp of the saints about, and the beloved city: and fire came down from God out of heaven and devoured them." –* **Revelation 20:9**

    b. Their rebellion fails. God lets the fire fall and it's all over.

    c. How foolish to fight against God.

    d. In an instant, they are cremated to a heap of ashes. No fowls are called to bury these that are dead.

The Doom of Satan

VI. THE DOOM OF SATAN – vs. 10

    a. *"And the devil that deceived them was cast into the lake of fire and brimstone, where the beast and the false prophet are, and shall be tormented day and night for ever and ever." –* **Revelation 20:10**

    b. The devil is cast into the lake of fire to join his two companions who have been there for a thousand years. Sinners are not annihilated in hell. While eternity rolls, you will never die.

The Last Judgment

I. THE JUDGE – vs. 11-15

    a. *"[11] And I saw a great white throne, and Him that sat on it, from whose face the earth and the heaven fled away; and there was found no place for them. [12] And I saw the dead, small and great, stand before God; and the books were opened: and another book was opened, which is the book of life: and the dead were judged out of those things which were written in the books, according to their works. [13] And the sea gave up the dead which were in it; and death and hell delivered up the dead which were in them: and they were judged every man according to their works. [14] And death and hell were cast into the lake of fire. This is the second death. [15] And whosoever was not found written in the book of life was cast into the lake of fire."* – Revelation 20:11-15

    b.   The One who the world has rejected and rebelled against, they will now stand before Him; the Judge of all judges.
        1.   Who is this Judge?
- He is the Son of the living God – **Matthew 16:16**
- *"For the Father judgeth no man, but hath committed all judgment unto the Son:"* – **John 5:22**
- He is:
  - ❖ The Judge – **Genesis 18:25**
  - ❖ The Just One – **Act 7:52**
  - ❖ A Jew – **John 4:9**
  - ❖ Jesus, the King – **I Timothy 1:17, 6:15, Matthew 21:5, Luke 19:38**

    c.   *"...and there was found no place for them."* – vs. 11
        1.   The sinners have no place to go but to the lake of fire.

II. THE JUDGED – vs. 12-13

    a.   *"[12] And I saw the dead, small and great, stand before God; and the books were opened: and another book was opened, which is the book of life: and the dead were judged out of those things which were written in the books, according to their works. [13] And the sea gave up the dead which were in it; and death and hell delivered up the dead which were in them: and they were judged every man according to their works."* – Revelation 20:12-13

    b.   *"And I saw the dead..."* – vs. 12
        1.   These dead here are unsaved.
        2.   Those unsaved are resurrected and brought to the final judgment in body and polluted soul.

- **John 5:28-29**
- **Act 24:15**
  - ❖ All of the righteous dead have previously been raised at the end of the first resurrection, 1000 years prior to this time in **Revelation 20:5**.

c. *"...small and great..."* – **vs. 12**
  1. The powerful
  2. The poor
  3. The rich
  4. The famous
  5. All the unsaved world

d. *"...stand before God..."* – **vs. 12**
  1. They continue to stand until judgment is done.

e. *"...and the books were opened..."* – **vs. 12**
  1. They were judged of those things that were written in the books according to their works.

f. *"...and another book was opened, which is the book of life..."* – **vs. 12**
  1. The Two Books
     - The Book of Life
       - ❖ The Book of Life, in time, contained every person's name born into this world. If a person rejects Christ and refuses to be saved and dies in their sins, then their name is removed from the Book of Life. They suffer the second death.
       - ❖ The reason their name is not in the Book of Life is because they are not saved.
       - ❖ The Book of Life along with the book of works will be used to determine the degree of punishment in hell.
         - The lost will be judged according to the light and opportunity they had.
           - ♦ **Matthew 10:11-15**
           - ♦ **Matthew 11:20-24**
           - ♦ **Luke 10:12-14**
           - ♦ **Luke 12:47-48**
       - ❖ To keep your name in the Book of Life, you must be born again.

- ❖ *"...Ye must be born again." – John 3:7*
- • The Lamb's Book of Life
  - ❖ The Lamb's Book of Life is the record of all those who have been born again.
  - ❖ At the moment of the new birth, your name is written in the Lamb's Book of Life.
  - ❖ No name is or can be blotted out of the Lamb's Book of Life because salvation is eternal.
    - **"[28] And I give unto them eternal life; and they shall never perish, neither shall any man pluck them out of My hand. [29] My Father, which gave them Me, is greater than all; and no man is able to pluck them out of My Father's hand." – John 10:28-29**
  2. Your record will be there. There will be no mistakes made.
- g. ***"And the sea gave up the dead which were in it..." – vs. 13***
  1. The sea holds the bodies of the unsaved who were buried or drowned in its waters.
- h. ***"...and death and hell delivered up the dead which were in them..." – vs. 13***
  1. Death holds the body in the grave.
  2. Hell holds the soul until the judgment of the unsaved. – **Revelation 20:13**

III. THE JUDGMENT – vs. 14-15

- a. *"[14] And death and hell were cast into the lake of fire. This is the second death. [15] And whosoever was not found written in the book of life was cast into the lake of fire." – Revelation 20:14-15*
- b. The records have been read and all are found guilty before God.
  1. Devotees of punishment

- ❖ Human beings created for heaven but went to hell.
2. Degree of punishment
   - ❖ The lake of fire and the second death.
3. Duration of punishment
   - ❖ **"*...for ever and ever...*" – Revelation 14:11**

If you are not saved, and you know that your name is not recorded in the Lamb's Book of Life, would you just bow your head and pray and say, *God, I know that I am a sinner. I now repent of my sins and ask You to come into my heart and life and save me. In Jesus Name I pray. Amen.*

***"For whosoever shall call upon the Name of the Lord shall be saved."* Romans 10:13**

Revelation – Chapter 21

The Dawn of the Eternal State

The New Heaven and the New Earth

I. **THE VISION** – vs. 1-2
    a. *"[1] And I saw a new heaven and a new earth: for the first heaven and the first earth were passed away; and there was no more sea. [2] And I John saw the holy city, new Jerusalem, coming down from God out of heaven, prepared as a bride adorned for her husband."* – Revelation 21:1-2
    b. *"Nevertheless we, according to His promise look for new heavens and a new earth, wherein dwelleth righteousness."* – II Peter 3:13
    c. *"…no more sea."* – vs. 1
        1. The sea is ever troublesome and restless, always on the move.
        2. It is a picture of the ungodly.
            • *"But the wicked are like the troubled sea…"* – Isaiah 57:20
        3. The sea divides continents. In the new heavens and the new earth, there will be no division or restlessness. All is calm and peaceful.

God With His People

II. **THE VOICE** – vs. 3
    a. *"And I heard a great voice out of heaven say, Behold, the tabernacle of God is with men, and He will dwell with them, and they shall be His people, and God Himself shall be with them, and be their God."* – Revelation 21:3

- b. The great voice out of heaven is the voice of the redeemed.
- c. The Blessing
  1. God with men
  2. Dwell with them
  3. Be their God
  4. *"Blessed are the pure in heart for they shall see God." – Matthew 5:8*

III. THE VICTOR AND THE VICTORY – vs. 4-8
- a. *"[4] And God shall wipe away all tears from their eyes; and there shall be no more death, neither sorrow, nor crying, neither shall there be any more pain: for the former things are passed away. [5] And He that sat upon the throne said, Behold, I make all things new. And He said unto me, Write: for these words are true and faithful. [6] And He said unto me, It is done. I am Alpha and Omega, the beginning and the end. I will give unto him that is athirst of the fountain of the water of life freely. [7] He that overcometh shall inherit all things; and I will be his God, and he shall be My son. [8] But the fearful, and unbelieving, and the abominable, and murderers, and whoremongers, and sorcerers, and idolaters, and all liars, shall have their part in the lake which burneth with fire and brimstone: which is the second death." – Revelation 21:4-8*
- b. Christ is the victor over all and every thing. He conquered death, hell, and the grave. He is King of kings and Lord of lords.
- c. The Saints victory is in Christ. – **vs. 4**
  1. *"But thanks be to God, which giveth us the victory through our Lord Jesus Christ." –* **I Corinthians 15:57**
     - No more tears – **vs. 4**
     - No more death – **vs. 4**
     - No more sorrow – **vs. 4**
     - No more crying – **vs. 4**
     - No more pain – **vs. 4**

REVELATION—CHAPTER 21

- "...the former things are passed away..." – **vs. 4**
- d. **"...all things new..." – vs. 5**
  1. We will move to a new home.
- e. The faithful Word – **vs. 5**
  1. These words are true and faithful.
  2. God will keep His promises to us.
- f. The settled fact – **vs. 6**
  1. **"...It is done." – vs. 6**
  2. It is done or accomplished, even as the same expression is heard in **Revelation 16:17** at the completion of the vial judgments. It is again heard at the completion of the new creation.
  3. Now all of God's promises to His people will also be completely fulfilled.
- g. **"...Alpha and Omega..." – vs. 6**
  1. Alpha and Omega are the first and last letters in the Greek alphabet, and here refers to the eternity of Christ.
- h. **"...the beginning and the end..." – vs. 6**
  1. This tells us that all testimony on the earth begin with God and will end with His glory.
- i. **"...I will give unto him that is athirst of the fountain of the water of life freely." – vs. 6**
  1. The Saints in heaven are satisfied and contented. There is free and abundant living water for all.
- j. The Overcomer – **vs. 7**
  1. As in Revelation chapters 2 and 3, the overcomer is the believer, the one who has drunk of the water of life. For him there is eternal sonship with God forever.

IV. THE VULGAR CROWD – vs. 8
  a. *"But the fearful, and unbelieving, and the abominable, and murderers, and whoremongers, and sorcerers, and idolaters, and all liars, shall have their part in the lake which burneth with fire and brimstone: which is the second death." –* **Revelation 21:8**
  b. The fearful

            1. They learned that Christianity required hardness, restraint, and restriction. They found it easier to drift with the tide than against it.
- c. The unbelieving
  1. Bold Christ rejecters
- d. The abominable
  1. This should be understood here in it's widest sense as denoting all that is morally, religiously, and physically filthy. – **Revelation 17:4-5, 21:27**
  2. Abominable means
     - Impure
     - Detesting
     - To be stinking
     - To be abhorred
- e. Murders
  1. Murders are groups like Judas, Hitler, Stalin, Saddam Hussein, and many other gangsters.
  2. It is a solemn thing to meddle with that which peculiarly belongs to God, that is human life.
- f. Whoremongers
  1. This points to a sin that is awfully prevalent. The ruin of female virtue is regarded lightly, and fornicators are received into society in the knowledge of the fact, while the poor victims are outcast from respectability. But God here reverses the judgment of man, and fornicators shall be consigned by the God of righteousness to the lake of fire.
- g. Sorcerers
  1. Sorcerer is the Greek word "Pharmakeia" which means pharmacy.
  2. Sorcerers are those who mix drugs with the practices of spirit worship, witchcraft, and magic. One writer has well described sorceries as misuse of drugs in connection with the occult.
  3. Oh that mankind would realize that it is the sole purpose of the world of demons to completely destroy the fair creation of God.

          4. Drugs can be used to heal or abuse. Today there is a worldwide abuse of drugs. May God help us!
   h. Idolaters
      1. These are all who worship other gods and images.
      2. This practice will be prevalent when the world bows to the anti-Christ's image. – **Revelation 13:11-18**
   i. Liars
      1. These are those who denied their sin and need of Christ as their Savior.
      2. Also it is those who habitually deceive others.

The Lamb's Wife: The New Jerusalem

V. THE DESCENDING CITY – vs. 9-10

   a. *"And there came unto me one of the seven angels which had the seven vials full of the seven last plagues, and talked with me, saying, Come hither, I will shew thee the bride, the Lamb's wife. [10] And he carried me away in the spirit to a great and high mountain, and shewed me that great city, the holy Jerusalem, descending out of heaven from God,"* – Revelation 21:9-10
   b. The angel revealed that he would show John **"the bride, the Lamb's wife" (vs. 9)**, which is identified as **"the holy Jerusalem, descending out of heaven from God." (vs. 10)**
      1. Why is the new Jerusalem called the bride, the wife of the Lamb?
         - The city is beautifully adorned, as will be the Church, Christ's bride at the marriage supper of the Lamb. – **Revelation 19:7**
         - The city will be spotless and pure, like Christ's Church after it is glorified.
            ❖ It should be understood that John is not saying that the bride is the New Jerusalem, but is being characterized

as the bride, the Lamb's wife. The bride is the Church. The city is the home of the Church.

VI. THE DESCRIPTION OF THE CITY – vs. 11-21

    a.   *"[11] Having the glory of God: and her light was like unto a stone most precious, even like a jasper stone, clear as crystal; [12] And had a wall great and high, and had twelve gates, and at the gates twelve angels, and names written thereon, which are the names of the twelve tribes of the children of Israel. [13] On the east three gates; on the north three gates; on the south three gates; and on the west three gates. [14] And the wall of the city had twelve foundations, and in them the names of the twelve apostles of the Lamb. [15] And he that talked with me had a golden reed to measure the city, and the gates thereof, and the wall thereof. [16] And the city lieth foursquare, and the length is as large as the breadth: and he measured the city with the reed, twelve thousand furlongs. The length and the breadth and the height of it are equal. [17] And he measured the wall thereof, and hundred and forty and four cubits, according to the measure of a man, that is, of the angel. [18] And the building of the wall of it was of jasper; and the city was pure gold, like unto clear glass. [19] And the foundations of the wall of the city were garnished with all manner of precious stones. The first foundation was jasper; the second, sapphire; the third, a chalcedony; the fourth, an emerald; [20] The fifth, sardonyx; the sixth, sardius; the seventh, chrysolyte; the eighth, beryl; the ninth, a topaz; the tenth, a chrysoprasus; the eleventh, a jacinth; the twelfth, an amethyst. [21] And the twelve gates were twelve pearls; every several gate was of one pearl: and the street of the city was pure gold, as it were transparent glass."* – Revelation 21:11-21

    b.   *"Having the glory of God..."* – vs. 11

        1.   Abraham looked for a city. – **Hebrews 11:10**

REVELATION—CHAPTER 21

- 2. This is a continuing city. – **Hebrews 13:14**
- c. **"...a wall great and high..." – vs. 12**
  - 1. This is symbolic of the glory of God.
  - 2. The Church needs, as it were, a wall of jasper.
    - The Saints are to reflect the glory of God now by living pure lives. And, in that day we will do it perfectly.
- d. **"...twelve gates..." – vs. 12-13**
  - 1. The names of the 12 tribes of Israel are written on the gates.
  - 2. Some say that God is through with Israel.
    - This is not so.
    - **"[1] I say, then, Hath God cast away His people? God forbid. For I also am an Israelite, of the seed of Abraham, of the tribe of Benjamin. [2] God hath not cast away His people which He foreknew..." – Romans 11:1-2**
- e. **"...twelve foundations..." – vs. 14**
  - 1. The names of the twelve apostles of the Lamb are ascribed upon those foundations.
  - 2. The 12 apostles laid the foundation for the Church upon the chief cornerstone, Christ Himself. – **Ephesians 2:20**
    - Not only are the 12 apostles represented, thus signifying the Church, but also, the 12 tribes of Israel. This suggests that both Church Saints and Old Testament Saints will find residence in the city.
- f. **"...the city lieth foursquare..." – vs. 15-17**
  - 1. The angel talks with John. – **vs. 15**
  - 2. A golden reed is a measuring rod of about 10 feet. – **vs. 15**
  - 3. The city is the new Jerusalem. – **vs. 15**
  - 4. The city, the gates, and the wall is the measuring of a beautiful place. – **vs. 15**
  - 5. **"...the city lieth foursquare..." – vs. 16**
    - This means the city was perfectly square.
    - The length is as large as the width. It is the same in each direction.
  - 6. **"...twelve thousand furlongs..." – vs. 16**

- Twelve thousand furlongs is equal to 1500 miles.
- The city is 1500 miles long, high, and wide.

7. The measurement of the wall. – **vs. 17**
   - **"...an hundred and forty and four cubits..."** – **vs. 17**
   - This is 216 feet high (based on a cubit being eighteen inches in length).
   - The wall is not for protection against evil. It is a glowing ornament of beauty and splendor.

g. The manner of the precious stones – **vs. 18-21**
   1. The wall – **vs. 18**
      - The wall of jasper and the city of pure gold will look like a sparkling diamond in all its crystalline beauty, designed to reflect the effulgence of God's radiant glory in every area of the city.
   2. The stones – **vs. 18**
      - Eight of the stones appear in the breastplate of the high priest **(Exodus 28:15-29)**. On each stone was engraved the name of one of the 12 tribes of Israel. And, as the high priest ministered before God, these names were upon his heart.
      - Christ knows us by name. We are precious to Him. – **vs. 19-20**
   3. The foundations – **vs. 19**
      - The city will have 12 foundations garnished with all manner of precious stones.
      - Each foundation will be made of the stones described in **verses 19-20**.
   4. The gates – **vs. 21**
      - The gates are of pearl. Pearls were highly valued in the ancient world for their natural beauty.
      - Each pearl gate will bear all the names of the 12 tribes of Israel and the gates will never be closed.
   5. The street – **vs. 21**

- The street of the city is pure gold, as it were transparent glass.
- This reminds us of God's righteousness that brought us salvation.

The New Temple

VII. THE DIRECT ACCESSIBLE WORSHIP OF GOD – vs. 22
    a.   *"And I saw no temple therein: for the Lord God Almighty and the Lamb are the temple of it." –* **Revelation 21:22**

    b.   Today we have great cathedrals that are suppose to symbolize the presence of God. Buildings are not the Church, nor do they prove that God's presence is there.

    c.   No temple – **vs. 22**
        1.   We will not need a special place to worship.
        2.   We will have immediate access to God.
- *"…the Lord God Almighty and the Lamb are the temple of it." –* **vs. 22**

The New Light

VIII. THE DIVINE LIGHT – vs. 23-26
    a.   *"[23] And the city had no need of the sun, neither of the moon, to shine in it: for the glory of God did lighten it, and the Lamb is the light thereof. [24] And the nations of them which are saved shall walk in the light of it: and the kings of the earth do bring their glory and honour into it. [25] And the gates of it shall not be shut at all by day: for there shall be no night there. [26] And they shall bring the glory and honour of the nations into it." –* **Revelation 21:23-26**

    b.   There will be no need of the sun or the moon to shine here. This does not mean there will not be any sun,

moon, or stars, but that their light will not be required to light the city.
 c. There will be a solar system in eternity. Read the following scriptures:
  1. **Psalm 75:5-17**
  2. **Psalm 89:36-37**
  3. **Psalm 148:3-6**
  4. **Jeremiah 31:35-36**
 d. *"God is light and in Him is no darkness at all." –* I John 1:5
 e. No secrets – **vs. 24**
  1. The saved shall walk in the light of it.
 f. Access – **vs. 25**
  1. The gates will never be closed.
 g. The Gentiles bring their glory and honor to God and the Lamb. – **vs. 26**
  1. Believers may seem to be very unimportant in this world today, but in heaven, it will be known how great they really are.

XI. <u>NO DEFILEMENT</u> – vs. 27

 a. *"And there shall in no wise enter into it any thing that defileth, neither whatsoever worketh abomination, or maketh a lie: but they which are written in the Lamb's book of life." –* **Revelation 21:27**
 b. No defilement can enter the city.
  1. No fallen angels or unbelievers will ever be there.
  2. Only God's blood washed believers whose names are written in the Lamb's Book of Life will be there.
  3. Is your name written there?

Revelation – Chapter 22

The New Paradise and It's River of the Water of Life

I. **THE RIVER** – vs. 1-2
    a. *"[1] And he shewed me a pure river of water of life, clear as crystal, proceeding out of the throne of God and of the Lamb. [2] In the midst of the street of it, and on either side of the river, was there the tree of life, which bare twelve manner of fruits, and yielded her fruit every month: and the leaves of the tree were for the healing of the nations."* – Revelation 22:1-2
    b. The river of water of life and the tree of life speaks of the fullness of life.
        1. *"They shall be abundantly satisfied with the fatness of thy house; and thou shalt make them drink of the river of thy pleasures."* – **Psalm 36:8**
        2. There will be no hunger, no thirst, no pollution, no germs or disease in heaven.

II. **THE REALITY** – vs. 3
    a. *"And there shall be no more curse: but the throne of God and of the Lamb shall be in it; and His servants shall serve Him:"* – Revelation 22:3
    b. Down here the saints groan and long to be free from the presence of sin **(Romans 8:23)**. In the new Jerusalem this becomes a reality.
    c. The curse of the Garden of Eden is gone. The curse began in **Genesis 3:14-19**.
    d. We will serve Him.
        1. There will be nothing to hamper believers in the service of God.
        2. Eternity will not be a place of idleness, boredom, or wearisome labor, but, one of joyful service and worship.

III. **THE RELATIONSHIP** – vs. 4
    a. *"And they shall see His face; and His name shall be in their foreheads."* – Revelation 22:4
    b. We are related to Jesus by blood and marriage.
        1. **Matthew 26:28**
        2. **Acts 20:28**
        3. **Romans 5:9**
        4. **I Peter 1:18-19**
        5. **Revelation 1:5**
        6. **Revelation 19:7-9**
    c. *"...they shall see His face..."* – vs. 4
        1. That face, once so vilely covered by the spittle of man, is now radiant with the glory of God.
        2. *"...and His name shall be in their foreheads."* – vs. 4
- This is the mark of
    - Redemption
    - Ownership

IV. **THE RULER AND RULERS** – vs. 5
    a. *"And there shall be no night there; and they need no candle, neither light of the sun; for the Lord God giveth them light: and they shall reign for ever and ever."* – Revelation 22:5
    b. There will be no night there. Darkness will be absent from the holy city, the New Jerusalem, forever. – **Revelation 21:23-25**
        1. *"The sun shall be no more thy light by day; neither for brightness shall the moon give light unto thee: but the Lord shall be unto thee an everlasting light, and thy God thy glory."* – Isaiah 60:19
    c. There is an idea that is misleading that says Christ's reign must end at the end of the 1000 years based upon I Corinthians 15:24-25. His reign does not end. It is the character of His reign that changes from the millennial reign to rule over the new heaven and the new earth and the saints reigning with Him in eternity. This is the eternal state.

V. THE RELIABILITY – vs. 6

a. *"And he said unto me, These sayings are faithful and true: and the Lord God of the holy prophets sent His angel to shew unto His servants the things which must shortly be done."* – **Revelation 22:6**

b. *"...These sayings are faithful and true..."* – **vs. 6**
   1. God's Word is faithful and true and will never pass away. – **Matthew 24:35**
   2. It is forever settled in heaven. – **Psalm 119:89**
   3. Faithful in the sense of its accuracy, reliability, and trustworthiness.
   4. True in the sense of being the whole truth from God.

c. *"...things which must shortly be done."* – **vs. 6**
   1. The word shortly means quickly and speedily.
   2. The point in time is not in view, but rather the period of time in which the events described in the book will take place with swiftness once they commence.

VI. THE RESULTS – vs. 7

a. *"Behold, I come quickly: blessed is he that keepeth the sayings of the prophecy of this book."* – **Revelation 22:7**

b. *"Behold, I come quickly..."* – **vs. 7**
   1. Christ's coming will be sudden.

c. *"...blessed is he that keepeth the sayings of the prophecy of this book."* – **vs. 7**
   1. Revelation begins with a blessing.
      - *"Blessed is he that readeth, and they that hear the words of this prophecy, and keep those things, which are written therein: for the time is at hand."* – **Revelation 1:3**
   2. Revelation ends with a blessing.
      - *"...blessed is he that keepeth the sayings of the prophecy of this book."* – **Revelation 22:7**

- "**Blessed are they that do His commandments...**" – Revelation 22:14
3. The word blessed means happy and content.
4. Those who keep the saying and the prophecy of this Book will be blessed, happy, and contented.

The Last Message of the Bible

VII. THE REFUSAL – vs. 8-9
a. *"[8] And I John saw these things, and heard them. And when I had heard and seen, I fell down to worship before the feet of the angel which shewed me these things. [9] Then saith he unto me, See thou do it not: for I am thy fellowservant, and of thy brethren the prophets, and of them which keep the sayings of this book: worship God."* – Revelation 22:8-9
b. The angel refuses John's worship.
   1. *"...See thou do it not..."* – vs. 9
   2. In all acts of worship, worship God only.

VIII. THE RETURN – vs. 10
a. *"And he saith unto me, Seal not the sayings of the prophecy of this book: for the time is at hand."* – Revelation 22:10
b. God commanded Daniel to shut up the words and seal the book even to the time of the end. – **Daniel 12:4**
c. God commanded John to seal not, meaning this is an open book.
d. In Daniel, the reason given was, the end then was afar off.
e. The reason given to John, for the time is at hand, refers to the second coming of Christ.

IX. **THE REBELLIOUS AND THE RIGHTEOUS – vs. 11**
   a. *"He that is unjust, let him be unjust still: and he which is filthy, let him be filthy still: and he that is righteous, let him be righteous still: and he that is holy, let him be holy still."* – **Revelation 22:11**
   b. Sinners have refused God and now they have a fixed destiny in hell for all eternity. There is no second chance. Nothing can change you in eternity.
   c. The righteous continue righteous and practice righteousness.
      1. The unjust
- Those who have not been justified by Christ

      2. The filthy
- The polluted ones

      3. The righteous
- Those that are born again

      4. The holy
- Speaks of being born again and an abundant spirit filled life

X. **THE REWARDS – vs. 12**
   a. *"And, behold, I come quickly; and My reward is with Me, to give every man according as his work shall be."* – **Revelation 22:12**
   b. Rewards for the New Testament Church Saints
      1. These will be given at the judgment seat of Christ, immediately after the rapture.
- **Romans 14:10**
- **I Corinthians 3:12-15**

   c. Rewards for the 12 Apostles
      1. These will be given at the administrative judgment of Israel in the millennium reign.
- **Matthew 19:28**

   d. Rewards for the Tribulation Saints
      1. Their reward is to live and reign with Christ for a 1000 years.
- **Revelation 20:4**

   e. Rewards for the Unsaved Dead

1. Their reward is the lake of fire.
   - Revelation 20:15

XI. THE REDEEMER AND THE REDEEMED – vs. 13-14

a. **"[13] I am Alpha and Omega, the beginning and the end, the first and the last. [14] Blessed are they that do His commandments, that they may have right to the tree of life, and may enter in through the gates into the city."** – Revelation 22:13-14

b. He is the Alpha and the Omega. – **vs. 13**
   1. There is nothing before or after Jesus Christ.

c. He is the beginning and the end. – **vs. 13**
   1. He is the one who created, controls, and will consummate all things.

d. He is the first and the last. – **vs. 13**
   1. He was before creation in eternity past and will be present in eternity future.

e. **"Blessed are they that do His commandments..."** – **vs. 14**
   1. Sinners do the Lord's commandments when they hear, repent, and obey the commandment to repent.
      - *"And the times of this ignorance God winked at; but now commandeth all men every where to repent."* – Acts 17:30
      - They are to repent and believe in Jesus Christ, at which point of obedience to Christ, they are saved, receive a pure heart, and become a child of God.
        - ❖ Acts 17:30-31
        - ❖ Galatians 3:26
        - ❖ Ephesians 2:8-9
        - ❖ Acts 15:9
      - Thereafter they are rewarded for obeying His commandments for holy living and divine service afterwards.
        - ❖ I Corinthians 3:8
        - ❖ I Corinthians 9:26-27
   2. Obedience to God's commandments is a true mark of our salvation.

REVELATION—CHAPTER 22

XII. **THE SINNERS** – vs. 15
    a. *"For without are dogs, and sorcerers, and whoremongers, and murderers, and idolaters, and whosoever loveth and maketh a lie." –* **Revelation 22:15**
    b. This is a special sin against God and mankind.
    c. When John speaks of dogs, he is not referring to the animal but to sinners of the lowest character. It is not at times they commit these sins, but that these are settled characteristics of their lives.
    d. The grace of God made their deliverance possible. They refused.

XIII. **THE SAVIOUR** – vs. 16
    a. *"I Jesus have sent mine angel to testify unto you these things in the churches. I am the root and the offspring of David, and the bright and morning star." –* **Revelation 22:16**
    b. Christ will inherit the throne of David. – **Luke 1:32**
        1. The offspring of David refers to the fact that Christ came into the world through the tribe of Judah. – **Genesis 49:10-11**
        2. David was from the tribe of Judah.
    c. To the Church, Christ will come as the bright and morning star. – **vs. 16**
    d. To Israel, He will come as the sun of righteousness with healing in His wings. – **Malachi 4:2**

XIV. **THE SALVATION INVITATION** – vs. 17
    a. *"And the spirit and the bride say, Come. And let him that heareth say, Come. And let him that is athirst come. And whosoever will, let him take the water of life freely." –* **Revelation 22:17**
    b. The Spirit – the Holy Spirit says come
    c. The Bride – the Church says come
    d. *"...let him that heareth..."* (vs. 17) – they say come
        1. Some will hear and say come to the Lord.
        2. They invite:
            • Their family

- Their friends
- Every one they meet

e. *"...let him that is athirst come."* (vs. 17)
   1. The desperate ones are invited.
f. *"...whosoever will..."* (vs. 17)
   1. The invitation extends to all.
g. *"...let him take the water of life freely."* (vs. 17)
   1. The water of life here is Jesus and eternal life.
   2. Freely means without price.
   3. The last call to come is urgent. The day will come when it will be too late to come.
   4. The day of opportunity will soon be over. Come to Jesus now.
      - *"[7] Wherefore as the Holy Ghost saith, To day if ye will hear His voice, [8] Harden not your hearts, as in the provocation, in the day of temptation in the wilderness:"* – Hebrews 3:7-8

XV. **THE SEVERITY** – vs. 18-19

a. *"[18] For I testify unto every man that heareth the words of the prophecy of this book, If any man shall add unto these things, God shall add unto him the plagues that are written in this book: [19] And if any man shall take away from the words of the book of this prophecy, God shall take away his part out of the book of life, and out of the holy city, and from the things which are written in this book."* – Revelation 22:18-19

b. This is a special warning to anyone who would add to or take away from this book. Anyone who does must suffer the consequences.
   1. To those who add to the book – **vs. 18**
      - The penalty for doing so will be to suffer the seal, the trumpet, and/or the vial judgments of the tribulation.
   2. To those who take away from the book – **vs. 19**
      - Of equal severity is the judgment upon those who take away from God's Word.

- This verse does not teach the loss of salvation.
- The pronouncement is to the unsaved who deny the scripture in the book regarding the Lord Jesus Christ.
- It is assured that those who deliberately add or take away from this book despise the Word of God, indicating they are not saved.
3. This warning, while it may refer specifically to Revelation, yet by a very true application, takes in the whole Bible.
4. Today, men who add or take away from the Word of God may not be judged like those in the tribulation period. But, they will surely be judged by God.

The Last Promise and Prayer of the Bible

XVI. **THE SURETY OF CHRIST'S COMING** – vs. 20-21

a. *"[20] He which testifieth these things saith, Surely I come quickly. Amen. Even so, come Lord Jesus. [21] The grace of our Lord Jesus Christ be with you all. Amen."* – Revelation 22:20-21
b. The Promise
1. *"…Surely I come quickly…"* – vs. 20
c. The Prayer
1. *"…Even so, come Lord Jesus."* – vs. 20
d. The Provision
1. *"The grace of our Lord Jesus Christ be with you all. Amen."* – vs. 21

A Word from the Author

Whether you meet Christ by way of death from this life into eternity, or whether you are one who may be living during these "Episodes of the End", every individual will meet the Lord Jesus Christ and spend eternity either in heaven or in hell.

Right now, if you are living in this world and have not accepted Jesus Christ as your personal Savior, you are in a very dangerous state in your life. If you don't accept the Lord Jesus Christ as your Savior, you could experience these end time judgements. If you would like to escape this terrible time that is to come, won't you follow these steps and receive the Lord Jesus into your heart.

Acknowledge that you are a sinner.

"For all have sinned, and come short of the glory of God." Romans 3:23

Believe that the Lord Jesus Christ was virgin born, died on the cross for your sins, rose again on the third day, and is coming again.

"Believe on the Lord Jesus Christ, and thou shalt be saved." Acts 16:31

Confess that Jesus Christ is Lord.

"That if thou shalt confess with thy mouth the Lord Jesus, and shalt believe in thine heart that God hath raised him from the dead, thou shalt be saved." Romans 10:9

REVELATION—CHAPTER 22

If God has spoken to your heart and you would like to be saved, if you will believe all of the above scripture and will pray the following prayer, God will give you the free gift of eternal life.

Dear Lord Jesus,

I know that I am a sinner and need Your forgiveness. I believe that You died on the cross for my sins, You arose on the third day, and that You are coming again. I ask that You come into my heart so that I may live eternally with You.

In Jesus' Name, Amen.

www.ingramcontent.com/pod-product-compliance
Lightning Source LLC
Chambersburg PA
CBHW062207080426
42734CB00010B/1831